JESUS:
THE EVIDENCE

PROF. ROBERT STEWART

V.F. WALKER PUBLISHING

ISBN-13 - 979-8510418279

Cover design by: Saira Artist
Printed in the United States of America

Title Page

Copyright Page

Contents

ROMAN DOCUMENTATION

There are many documents regarding the life of the Jesus of two-thousand years ago that have been either *undiscovered* and buried in the earth or *discovered* and *purposely deleted* from The Bible; the later *(intentional deletions and distortions by white Jews, Romans, Greeks, English, and others)* most aptly applies. Consequently, it is near impossible, in this modern day, to ascertain the *complete truth* regarding Jesus. Therefore, I'm forced to rely upon *scriptural corroborative evidence*. Hopefully, this will deliver at least some form of *cohesion* to the gargantuan puzzle that has been *purposely created* by the aforementioned parties. That being said, I will predominately use the *King James Version* of The Bible (of the year 1611), and the *Maulana Muhammad Ali* English translation of The Holy Qur'an of Islam (of the year 1917). There are many other alleged scriptures or documents in existence that deliver not only a large portion of *missing information* regarding the life of Jesus, but *many other prophets* or servants of The Lord as well.

A few of these documents include: *The Apocrypha (meaning hidden or secret), The Forgotten Books of Eden, The Gospel of Mary, The Gospel of Thomas, The Gospel of Bartholomew*, and many others. Unfortunately, most adherents to Christianity *ignorantly* believe that *only the 66 books of the King James Bible* are the actual "Word of God." Consequently, I will entertain their misinformed assertion by using the King James Version *predominately, but not exclusively.*

The primary question asked most often today is did Jesus actually exist? The answer is that there is circumstantial evidence for his existence offered by these ancient Romans:

1. Roman Governor Pliny The Younger wrote a letter to Emperor Trajan stating that Christians would "sing hymns to Christ as to a god."

2. Roman Historian Suetonius wrote that Emperor Claudius expelled Jews from Rome for "making constant disturbances at the instigation of Chrestus (Christ)."

3. In the <u>Annals of Imperial Rome</u> (written in 116 A.D.), Roman Senator Tacitus wrote: "Emperor Nero blamed the persons commonly called Christians. Christus (Christ), the founder of the name, was put to death by Pontius Pilate in the reign of Tiberius."

Consequently, it is extremely unlikely that these ranking Roman citizens would be concocting a fictious account about a fictious man whom the Jews called Christ (meaning *anointed*). Let us now consult the Bible for the birth of the man called Christ:

THE HOLY SPIRIT (VIRGIN BIRTH)

Bible / Matthew 1

18. Now the birth of Jesus Christ was on this wise: When as his mother Mary was espoused to Joseph, before they came together, *she was found with child of the Holy Ghost.*

19. Then Joseph her husband, being a just man, and not willing to make her a public example, was minded to put her away privily.

20. But while he thought on these things, behold, the angel of The Lord appeared unto him in a dream, saying, Joseph, thou son of David, fear not to take unto thee Mary thy wife: for that which is conceived in her is of the Holy Ghost.

21. And she shall bring forth a son, and thou shalt call his name JESUS: for he shall save his people from their sins.

22. Now all this was done, that it might be fulfilled which was spoken of The Lord by the prophet, saying,

23. Behold, *a virgin shall be with child*, and shall bring forth a son, and *they shall call his name Emmanuel*, which being interpreted is, *God with us*.

The Lord miraculously produced children *from the wombs of barren (unable to conceive) women on numerous occasions before the birth of Jesus. Sarai* (wife of Abraham), *Rebekah* (wife of Isaac), and *Rachel* (wife of Jacob) were all stricken with barrenness, yet *miraculously* conceived upon The Lord's command. Although Mary's *virginity* grants her a distinction from the aforementioned, her child's *(Jesus)* "Holy Ghost" is *NOT distinctive or exclusive*. In fact, Mary's *blood-cousin Elisabeth* had a child of *the same Holy Ghost as Jesus*:

Bible / Luke 1

5. THERE was in the days of Herod, the king of Judaea, a certain priest named *Zacharias*, of the course of Abia: and his wife was of the daughters of Aaron, and her name was *Elisabeth*.

6. And they were both righteous before God, walking in all the commandments and ordinances of The Lord blameless.

7. And they had no child, because that *Elisabeth was barren, and they both were now well stricken in years*.

13. But the angel said unto him, Fear not, Zacharias: for thy prayer is heard; and thy wife Elisabeth *shall bear thee a son*, and thou shalt call his name *John*.

14. And thou shalt have joy and gladness; and many shall rejoice at his birth.

15. For he shall be great in the sight of The Lord, and shall drink neither wine nor strong drink; and he shall *be filled with the Holy Ghost*, even from his mother's womb.

16. And many of the children of Israel shall he turn to The Lord their God.

18. And Zacharias said unto the angel, Whereby shall I know this? for I am an old man, and my wife well stricken in years.

19. And the angel answering said unto him, *I am Gabriel*, that stand in the presence of God; and am sent to speak unto thee, and to shew thee these glad tidings.

24. And after those days his wife *Elisabeth conceived*, and hid herself five months, saying,

25. Thus hath The Lord dealt with me in the days wherein he looked on me, *to take away my reproach among men.*

After delivering these declarations to Elisabeth's husband (Zacharias), arch-angel *Gabriel* (often referred to as *The Holy Spirit or Holy Ghost*) was commanded by The Lord to deliver the *same good news* of a divine child to Elisabeth's cousin, *Mary*:

Bible / Luke 1

36. And, behold, *thy cousin Elisabeth*, she hath *also conceived* a son in her old age: and this is the sixth month with her, *who was called barren.*

37. For with God *nothing shall be impossible*.

39. And Mary arose in those days, and went into the hill country with haste, into a city of Juda;

40. And entered into the house of Zacharias, and saluted Elisabeth.

41. And it came to pass, that, when Elisabeth heard the salutation of Mary, the babe leaped in her womb; and *Elisabeth was filled with the Holy Ghost*:

42. And she spake out with a loud voice, and said, Blessed art thou among women, and *blessed is the fruit of thy womb*.

43. And whence is this to me, that the mother of my Lord should come to me?

44. Or, lo, as soon as the voice of thy salutation sounded in mine ears, the babe leaped in my womb for joy.

45. And blessed is she that believed: for there shall be a performance of those things which were told her from The Lord.

46. And Mary said, My soul doth magnify The Lord,

63. And he (Zacharias) asked for a writing table, and wrote, saying, *His name is John*. And they marveled all.

Consequently, the Holy Ghost or Holy Spirit is *NOT exclusively owned by Jesus*, whatsoever. Actually, other men were *filled with the same Holy Ghost or Spirit* millenniums before the births of Jesus and John:

Bible / Exodus 35

30. And Moses said unto the children of Israel, See, The Lord hath called by name *Bezaleel* the son of Uri, the son of Hur, of the tribe of Judah;

31. And he hath *filled him with the spirit of God*, in wisdom, in understanding, and in knowledge, and in all manner of workmanship.

Bible / Job 33

4. The *spirit of God hath made me (Elihu)*, and the breath of the Almighty hath given me life.

As is plain, the Holy Ghost or Spirit is *NOT exclusively owned by Jesus* in the least. The primary distinction between Jesus and other servants of The Lord is that *his mother was a virgin*. The Holy Qur'an confirms the birth of Jesus from a virgin, thusly:

Holy Qur'an / Surah 3

45. When the angels said: O Mary, surely Allah gives thee good news with a word from Him (of one) whose name is the Messiah, <u>*Jesus*</u>, son of *Mary*, worthy of regard in this world and the Hereafter, and of those who are drawn nigh (to Allah),

46. And he will speak to the people when in the cradle and when of old age, and (he will be) of the good ones.

47. She said: My Lord, how can I have a son and *man has not yet touched me?* He said: Even so; Allah creates what He pleases. When He decrees a matter, *He only says to it, Be, and it is.*

48. And He will teach him the Book and the Wisdom and the Torah and the Gospel.

Holy Qur'an / Surah 19

16. And mention Mary in the Book. When she drew aside from her family to an eastern place;

17. So she screened herself from them. Then We sent to her *Our spirit* and it appeared to her *as a well-made man*.

18. She said: I flee for refuge from thee to the Beneficent, if thou art one guarding against evil.

19. He said: I am only bearer of a message of thy Lord: That I will give thee a pure boy.

20. She said: How can I have a son and *no mortal has yet touched me, nor have I been unchaste*?

21. He said: So (it will be). Thy Lord says: It is easy to Me; and that *We may make him a sign to men* and a mercy from Us. And it is a matter decreed.

22. Then she conceived him; and withdrew with him to a remote place.

Holy Qur'an / Surah 3

59. The *likeness of Jesus* with Allah is truly as the *likeness of Adam*. He created him from dust, then said to him, *Be, and he was*.

60. (This is) the truth from thy Lord, so be not of the disputers.

Consequently, the birth of Jesus from a virgin mother is "a sign to men," as verse 21 of Surah 19 clearly states. The sign being that The Lord of the Universe *can accomplish anything that he desires*; even override his natural procreation law.

<u>MARY & JOSEPH ESCAPE INTO EGYPT</u>

Bible / Matthew 2

13. And when they were departed, behold, the angel of The Lord appeareth to Joseph in a dream, saying, Arise, and take the young child and his mother, and *flee into Egypt*, and be thou there until I bring thee word: for Herod will seek the young child to destroy him.

14. When he arose, he took the young child and his mother by night, and *departed into Egypt*:

15. And was there until the death of Herod: that it might be fulfilled which was spoken of The Lord by the prophet, saying, *Out of Egypt have I called my son!*

Firstly, The Lord of the Worlds *has no single human son.* This rhetoric was *concocted and inserted* by human demons in skin suits. Secondly, the "Out of Egypt have I called my son" terminology in verse 15 of Matthew 2, is in *symbolic reference to an entire nation (not a single individual) of Jews, and their exodus from Egypt.* The prophet relaying this information is alleged to be *Hosea*:

Bible / Hosea 11

1. When *Israel* was a child, then I loved him, and *called my son out of Egypt.*

2. As they called them, *so they went from them*: they sacrificed unto Baalim, and burned incense to graven images.

As is apparent in the preceding verses, *Hosea is metaphorically referring to the Nation of Israel (not Jesus) as the son or child of God who was called out of Egypt.* The words of the prophet *Moses* also corroborate this:

Bible / Exodus 13

8. And thou shalt shew *thy son* in that day, saying, This is done because of that which The Lord *did unto me* when *I came forth out of Egypt.*

15. And it came to pass, when Pharaoh would hardly let us go, that The Lord slew all the firstborn in the land of Egypt, both the firstborn of man, and the firstborn of beast: therefore I sacrifice to The Lord all that openeth the matrix, being males; but all the firstborn of *my children* I redeem.

16. And it shall be for a token upon thine hand, and for frontlets between thine eyes: for by strength of hand The Lord *brought us forth out of Egypt.*

The term *Israel* means "he strives with God and prevails." This name was originally given to *Jacob (son of Isaac, grandson of Abraham)* by an angel of The Lord:

Bible / Genesis 32

28. And he said, Thy name shall be called *no more Jacob*, but *ISRAEL*: for as a prince hast *thou power with God* and with men, and hast *prevailed*.

Since the *Nation of Israel* is of the lineage or seed of Jacob, they simply *adopted his new name*. Hence, Jesus is *never referred to as "Israel" anywhere in The Bible*. Consequently, the "when Israel was a child, then I loved him, and called my son out of Egypt" prophesy of *Hosea*, is in reference to *the entire seed or nation of Jacob, not a single individual*. This was once crystal clear before demons in human skin suits *distorted* the plain truth from The Lord of the Worlds.

CHILDHOOD – ADOLESCENCE

Regarding the *childhood or adolescence of Jesus*, not much is relayed in The Bible. In fact, The Bible has *18 entire years of Jesus' life missing*:

Bible / Luke 2

41. Now his parents went to Jerusalem every year at the feast of the passover.

42. And when *he was twelve years old*, they went up to Jerusalem after the custom of the feast.

Bible / Luke 3

23. And Jesus himself *began to be about thirty years of age*, being (as was supposed) the son of Joseph, which was the son of Heli.

Yeah, demons disguised in human skin suits have *REMOVED* the information from The Bible regarding the childhood and early adulthood (18 years) of Jesus. There is only one instance in The Bible where Jesus is manifesting thc wisdom of The Lord *as a child*:

40. And the child grew, and waxed strong in spirit, *filled with wisdom*: and the grace of God was upon him.

46. And it came to pass, that after three days they found him in the temple, sitting in the midst of the doctors, both hearing them, and asking them questions.

47. And all that heard him were astonished at his *understanding and answers*.

48. And when they saw him, *they were amazed*: and his mother said unto him, Son, why hast thou thus dealt with us? behold, thy father and I have sought thee sorrowing.

49. And he said unto them, How is it that ye sought me? wist ye not that *I must be about my Father's business?*

What was Jesus doing *before he was 30 years of age*, and why was this information *removed from The Bible?* Fortunately, other scriptures exist to provide insight:

Holy Qur'an / Surah 5

110. When Allah will say: O Jesus, son of Mary, remember My favour to thee and to thy mother, when I strengthened thee with the Holy Spirit; thou spokest to people in the cradle and in old age, and when I taught thee the Book and the Wisdom and the Torah and the Gospel, and when thou didst determine *out of clay a thing like the form of a bird* by My permission, then thou didst breathe into it and it became a bird by My permission; and

thou didst heal the blind and the leprous by My permission; and when thou didst raise the dead by My permission; and when I withheld the Children of Israel from thee when thou camest to them with clear arguments – but those of them who disbelieved said: This is nothing but clear enchantment.

The Infancy Gospel of Thomas

1. I, Thomas the Israelite, tell unto you, even all the brethren that are of the Gentiles, to make known unto you the *works of the childhood of our Lord Jesus* Christ and his mighty deeds, even all that he did when he was born in our land: whereof the beginning is thus:

2. This little child Jesus when he was *five years old* was playing at the ford of a brook: and he gathered together the waters that flowed there into pools, and made them straightway clean, and commanded them by his word alone. And having *made soft clay, he fashioned thereof twelve sparrows*. And it was the Sabbath when he did these things (or made them). And there were also many other little children playing with him.

3. And a certain Jew when he saw what Jesus did, playing upon the Sabbath day, departed straightway and told his father Joseph: Lo, thy child is at the brook, and *he hath taken clay and fashioned twelve little birds*, and hath polluted the Sabbath day.

4. And Joseph came to the place and saw: and cried out to him, saying: Wherefore doest thou these things on the Sabbath, which it is not lawful to do? But Jesus clapped his hands together and cried out to the sparrows and said to them: *Go! And the sparrows took their flight* and went away chirping.

5. And when the Jews saw it they were amazed, and departed and told their chief men that which they had seen Jesus do.

Again, there are *other documents in existence* regarding the childhood deeds of Jesus that were *omitted from The Bible*. In fact, _Eusebius_ lived from 260 to 339 AD and is the _founding father of Church history_ with his writing, Ecclesiastical History. _St. Jerome_ (342-347 to 420 AD) was a theologian and translator of The Vulgate (Latin Bible). Both men relayed doubts regarding the precise translations of The Bible, because they were *witnesses* of scribes inserting their personal interpretations or opinions, rather than simply delivering the *verbatim words* of scripture. So, my claim of the current Bibles of the globe being purposely distorted is actual fact according to the founders of Christian church history.

Here is an omitted account of the *vengeful* and *murderous* Jesus.

The Gospel of Thomas

(The Infancy of Jesus) / Chapter 2

2. But the boy Jesus seeing what he had done, became angry, and said to him, Thou fool, what harm did the lake do thee, that thou shouldest scatter the water?

3. Behold, now thou shalt *wither as a tree*, and shalt not bring forth either leaves, or branches, or fruit.

4. And immediately he became *withered all over*.

5. Then Jesus went away home. But the parents of the boy who was withered, lamenting the misfortune of his youth, took and carried him to Joseph, accusing him, and said, *Why dost thou keep a son who is guilty of such actions*?

6. Then Jesus at the request of all who were present did heal him, *leaving only some small member to continue withered, that they might take warning*.

7. Another time Jesus went forth into the street, and a boy running by, rushed upon his shoulder;

8. At which *Jesus being angry, said to him, thou shalt go no farther.*

9. *And he instantly fell down dead:*

10. Which when some persons saw, they said, Where was this boy born, that everything which he says presently cometh to pass?

11. Then the parents of the dead boy going to Joseph complained, saying, You are not fit to live with us, in our city, having such a boy as that:

12. Either teach him that he bless and not curse, or else depart hence with him, for *he kills our children.*

13. Then Joseph calling the boy Jesus by himself, instructed him saying, Why doest thou such things to injure the people so, that they hate us and prosecute us?

14. But Jesus replied, I know that what thou sayest is not of thyself, but for thy sake I will say nothing;

15. But they who have said these things to thee, *shall suffer everlasting punishment.*

16. And immediately they who had accused him *became blind.*

17. And all they who saw it were exceedingly afraid and confounded, and said concerning him, Whatsoever he saith,

whether good or bad, immediately cometh to pass: and they were amazed.

Aye, in the Bible book of Matthew 21 verse 19, Jesus *killed a fig tree* because he was hungry but the tree had no figs. *It withered the same as the boy* in the preceding verses. Let us now focus upon *the deeds of the adult Jesus*.

JESUS THE ADULT

Bible / Matthew 4

23. And Jesus went about all Galilee, teaching in their synagogues, and preaching the gospel of the kingdom, and *healing all manner of sickness* and all manner of disease among the people.

24. And his fame went throughout all Syria: and they brought unto him all sick people that were taken with divers diseases and torments, and those which were *possessed with devils*, and those which were lunatick, and those that had the palsy; and *he healed them*.

Bible / Mark 1

23. And there was in their synagogue a man with an *unclean spirit*; and he cried out,

24. Saying, Let us alone; what have we to do with thee, thou Jesus of Nazareth? art thou come to destroy us? I know thee who thou art, *the Holy One of God*.

25. And Jesus rebuked him, saying, Hold thy peace, and come out of him.

26. And when the unclean spirit had torn him, and cried with a loud voice, he came out of him.

In verse 24 of Mark 1, notice that the unclean spirit (demon) *knew the true identity of Jesus; the holy one OF God, not God himself.* This is a colossal decree, for this single verse makes *worshiping Jesus completely illogical. Jesus did not tell a single soul (anywhere in The Bible) to worship or pray to him;* more on this later:

Bible / Matthew 9

20. And, behold, a woman, which was diseased with an issue of blood twelve years, came behind him, and touched the hem of his garment:

21. For she said within herself, If I may but touch his garment, I shall be whole.

22. But Jesus turned him about, and when he saw her, he said, Daughter, be of good comfort; *thy faith hath made thee whole.* And the woman was made whole from that hour.

23. And when Jesus came into the ruler's house, and saw the minstrels and the people making a noise,

24. He said unto them, Give place: for the maid is not dead, but sleepeth. And they laughed him to scorn.

25. But when the people were put forth, he went in, and took her by the hand, and *the maid arose*.

26. And the fame hereof went abroad into all that land.

27. And when Jesus departed thence, two blind men followed him, crying, and saying, Thou son of David, have mercy on us.

28. And when he was come into the house, the blind men came to him: and Jesus saith unto them, *Believe ye that I am able to do this?* They said unto him, Yea, Lord.

29. Then touched he their eyes, saying, *According to your faith be it unto you*.

30. And their eyes were opened; and Jesus straitly charged them, saying, *See that no man know it*.

31. But they, when they were departed, *spread abroad his fame in all that country*.

Notice in verse 22 of Matthew 9, Jesus told the woman that *her faith* had cured her of her ailment; the same he relayed to the blind men in verse 29. Jesus was *merely a humble servant* of The Creator and Master of the Universe, *Jehovah*. Consequently, *his own faith in Lord Jehovah* allowed him to accomplish his marvelous miracles; Al Hamduli llah. [English: All praise is due to God] Further, the "see that no man know it" command from Jesus in verse 30, is a testament of *his tremendous humility when in the presence of non-enemies*. However, this humility could *instantaneously transform into fierce wrath or indignation toward those whom he deemed to be enemies.* Or simply, he exemplified the *positive and negative (duality)* inherent in "The Real Mind of God."

Bible / John 11

39. Jesus said, Take ye away the stone. Martha, the sister of him that was dead, saith unto him, Lord, by this time he stinketh: for he hath been *dead four days*.

40. Jesus saith unto her, Said I not unto thee, that, if thou wouldest believe, thou shouldest see the glory of God?

41. Then they took away the stone from the place where the dead was laid. And Jesus lifted up his eyes, and said, Father, *I thank thee* that thou hast heard me.

42. And I knew that thou hearest me always: but because of the people which stand by I said it, that they may believe that *thou hast sent me*.

43. And when he thus had spoken, he cried with a loud voice, Lazarus, come forth.

44. And he that was *dead came forth*, bound hand and foot with graveclothes: and his face was bound about with a napkin. Jesus saith unto them, Loose him, and let him go.

PROPHETHOOD OF JESUS

Bible / Luke 7

12. Now when he came nigh to the gate of the city, behold, there was a *dead man* carried out, the only son of his mother, and she was a widow: and much people of the city was with her.

13. And when The Lord saw her, he had compassion on her, and said unto her, Weep not.

14. And he came and touched the bier: and they that bare him stood still. And he said, Young man, I say unto thee, *Arise*.

15. And *he that was dead sat up, and began to speak*. And he delivered him to his mother.

16. And there came a fear on all: and they glorified God, saying, That a *great prophet* is risen up among us; and, That God hath visited his people.

The colossal significance of the preceding is not only that Jesus gave life to the *presumed* dead (by The Lord's permission), but that there were some *who knew that he was merely a prophet* of The Lord. Consequently, there are *fragments* of actual truth within The Bible. The Holy Qur'an also confirms the *prophet-hood* of Jesus:

Holy Qur'an / Surah 19

27. Then she came to her people with him, carrying him. They said: O Mary, thou has indeed brought a strange thing!

28. O sister of Aaron, thy father was not a wicked man, nor was thy mother an unchaste woman!

29. But she pointed to him. They said: How should we speak to one who is a child in the cradle?

30. He said: I am indeed *a servant* of Allah. He has given me the Book and *made me a prophet*:

31. And He has made me blessed wherever I may be, and He has enjoined on me prayer and poor-rate so long as I live:

32. And to be kind to my mother; and He has not made me insolent, unblessed.

33. And peace on me the day I was born, and the day I die, and the day I am raised to life.

34. *Such is Jesus* son of Mary - a statement of truth about which they dispute.

Holy Qur'an / Surah 5

75. The Messiah, son of Mary, was *only a messenger*; Messengers before him had indeed passed away. And his mother was a truthful woman. They both used to eat food. See how We make the messages clear to them! Then behold, how they are turned away!

In light of this, *praying to any mere mortal* human prophet of The Lord (Jesus included) is *blasphemy and void of sanity*, indeed. Jesus was a *prophet and messenger* of The Lord of the Universe, nothing more. Let us now address *the environmental miracles of Jesus*:

ENVIRONMENTAL MIRACLES

23. And when he was entered into a ship, his disciples followed him.

24. And, behold, there arose a great tempest in the sea, insomuch that the ship was covered with the waves: but he was asleep.

25. And his disciples came to him, and awoke him, saying, Lord, save us: we perish.

26. And he saith unto them, Why are ye fearful, O ye of *little faith*? Then he arose, and *rebuked the winds and the sea; and there was a great calm.*

27. But the men *marveled*, saying, What manner of man is this, that *even the winds and the sea obey him!*

25. And in the fourth watch of the night Jesus went unto them, *walking on the sea.*

26. And when the disciples saw him walking on the sea, they were troubled, saying, It is a spirit; and they cried out for fear.

27. But straightway Jesus spake unto them, saying, Be of good cheer; it is I; be not afraid.

28. And Peter answered him and said, Lord, if it be thou, bid me *come unto thee on the water*.

29. And he said, Come. And when Peter was come down out of the ship, *he walked on the water*, to go to Jesus.

30. But when he saw the wind boisterous, *he was afraid*; and beginning to sink, he cried, saying, Lord, save me.

31. And immediately Jesus stretched forth his hand, and caught him, and said unto him, *O thou of little faith, wherefore didst thou doubt*?

Bible / Matthew 17

1. And after six days Jesus taketh Peter, James, and John his brother, and bringeth them up into an high mountain apart,

2. And was *transfigured* before them: and his *face did shine* as the sun, and his *raiment was white as the light*.

3. And, behold, there appeared unto them *Moses and Elias talking with him*.

Bible / Matthew 21

18. Now in the morning as he returned into the city, *he hungered*.

19. And when he saw a fig tree in the way, he came to it, and *found nothing thereon*, but leaves only, and said unto it, *Let no fruit grow on thee henceforward forever*. And presently the fig tree *withered away*.

20. And when the disciples saw it, *they marveled*, saying, How soon is the fig tree withered away!

21. Jesus answered and said unto them, Verily I say unto you, If *ye have faith, and doubt not*, ye shall not only *do this* which is done to the fig tree, but also if ye shall say unto *this mountain, Be thou removed*, and be thou *cast into the sea; it shall be done*.

22. And all things, whatsoever ye shall ask in prayer, *believing*, ye shall receive.

JESUS THE SINNER

Jesus *stopped a storm, walked on water, conversed with the astral or spirit forms of the prophets Moses and Elias (Greek name for Elijah), and killed an innocent fig tree in a moment of rage or indignation*. While his disciples were busy marveling at his deeds, they missed or simply *disregarded* his greatest decree to them, *FAITH*. Yeah, if they had only *believed (void of doubt)*, they could have *also done that which Jesus had done*. Hence, Jesus *never elevated himself above other mortal human beings who were not his enemies*, whatsoever. It was his *chronically defiant - rebellious disciples* (and others who were around him) who *chose to worship or deify him*. Jesus *despised this* according to The Bible and Holy Qur'an. In fact, Jesus knew himself *to be a sinner, the same as all mere mortal men are sinners*; no matter how holy they *appear or proclaim* themselves to be. Actually, a sin of Jesus is within verse 19 of Matthew 21: "Let no fruit grow on thee henceforward forever. And presently the fig tree withered away." Consequently, since *he killed the innocent tree,* he was *guilty of breeching one of the commandments of Moses* from Lord Jehovah: "*Thou shalt not kill.*" Outburst such as the aforementioned was the reason that Jesus *hated being worshipped or deified*. Here is corroborative evidence of *his disdain for praise*:

Bible / Luke 18

18. And a certain ruler asked him, saying, *Good Master,* what shall I do to inherit eternal life?

19. And Jesus said unto him, *Why callest thou me good? none is good, save one, that is, God.*

20. Thou knowest the commandments, Do not commit adultery, *Do not kill,* Do not steal, Do not bear false witness, Honour thy father and thy mother.

Yeah, Jesus *never proclaimed himself to be sinless at any time*. Therefore, how in sanity can Jesus be *Jehovah or God himself,* if he does not even desire to be *referred to as good,* eh? Alleged Christians *have exceeded divine limits* in their proclaiming Jesus to be *sinless*. Further, *his killing of a living thing (fig tree) makes him a sinner,* and *no greater than any other mortal human being of fallacies*. Here is another manifest *fallacy of Jesus*:

Bible / Leviticus 10

8. And The Lord spake unto Aaron, saying,

33

9. *Do not drink wine nor strong drink*, thou, nor thy sons with thee, when ye go into the tabernacle of the congregation, lest ye die: it shall be a statute for ever throughout your generations:

10. And that ye may put difference between *holy and unholy*, and between *unclean and clean*;

Bible / Proverbs 20

1. *Wine* is a mocker, *strong drink* is raging: and whosoever is deceived thereby is *not wise*.

Bible / Matthew 11

18. For John came neither eating nor drinking, and they say, He hath a devil.

19. The Son of man came eating and drinking, and they say, Behold a man *gluttonous*, and a *wine-bibber*, a friend of *publicans* and *sinners*. But wisdom is justified of her children.

Bible / John 4

46. So Jesus came again into Cana of Galilee, where *he made the water wine*. And there was a certain nobleman, whose son was sick at Capernaum.

It is blatantly obvious that in *Leviticus 10* (although it refers to the tabernacle), Jehovah declares *wine and stronger drinks to be unholy and unclean*. Therefore, if verse 46 of John 4 is true, would not the transformation of *water into that which*

is unholy and unclean be a manifest sin of Jesus? The Holy
Qur'an corroborates Lord Jehovah's decree regarding *intoxicants*:

Holy Qur'an / Surah 5

90. O you who believe, *intoxicants and games of chance* and
(sacrificing to) stones set up and (dividing by) arrows are only
an *uncleanness, the devil's work; so shun it* that you may
succeed.

91. The devil desires only to create enmity and hatred among you
by means of intoxicants and games of chance, and to keep you
back from the remembrance of Allah and from prayer. Will you
then keep back?

Consequently, Jesus *was no greater than any other mortal
human being of fallacies,* whatsoever. However, he did not
condone or approve of wrongdoing. This is evident in his *rage
and indignation* against the *moneychangers,* and others within the
temple:

Bible / Matthew 21

11. And the multitude said, This is *Jesus the prophet* of
Nazareth of Galilee.

12. And Jesus went into the temple of God, and *cast out all them*
that sold and bought in the temple, and *overthrew the tables* of
the moneychangers, and *the seats of them that sold doves,*

13. And said unto them, It is written, My house shall be called
the house of prayer; but ye have made it *a den of thieves.*

Aside from the multitude knowing that Jesus was *merely a prophet* (rather than *Jehovah - God himself*), they were present to witness his *display of rage*. So, if this occurrence is true, alleged Christians should cease their rebellious quest to transform that *colossal soldier of stern resolve against the enemies of The Lord, into a timid little punk who allowed folks to knock him in the head or put their feet in his behind*. The *Jesus of Rage* in the preceding verses was hardly teaching anyone to: "*Love thy enemies, bless those that curse you, turn the other cheek,*" and the rest of those *utterly ridiculous* bumper-sticker slogans that have been *diabolically inserted* into The Bible *by demons* of Satan housed in human skin suits. I will address this subject in greater detail later in this book. Let us return to the *subject of sin, and the reactions of Jesus toward such*:

Bible / John 8

3. And the scribes and Pharisees brought unto him a woman taken in adultery; and when they had set her in the midst,

4. They say unto him, Master, this woman was taken in adultery, in the very act.

5. Now Moses in the law commanded us, that such should be stoned: but what sayest thou?

6. This they said, *tempting him*, that they might have to accuse him. But Jesus stooped down, and with his finger *wrote on the ground*, as though *he heard them not*.

7. So when they continued asking him, he lifted up himself, and said unto them, He that is *without sin among you*, let him first cast a stone at her.

8. And again he stooped down, and *wrote on the ground*.

9. And they which heard it, being *convicted by their own conscience*, went out one by one, beginning at the eldest, even unto the last: and Jesus was left alone, and the woman standing in the midst.

10. When Jesus had lifted up himself, and saw none but the woman, he said unto her, Woman, where are those thine accusers? hath no man condemned thee?

11. She said, No man, Lord. And Jesus said unto her, *Neither do I condemn thee: go, and sin no more.*

The Jesus depicted here *is not timid or meek, but absolutely fearless, and as ornery or defiant as any prophet of The Lord that came before him*. Notice that the *Pharisees* (English: *To separate or separatists*) *insidiously* attempted to force him to defy the laws of The Lord delivered by Moses. However, Jesus (knowing that *egomaniacs despise being ignored*) began doodling on the ground in *open rebellion* as they spoke. Actually, his victory over the egomaniac Pharisees was twofold, for his verbal response: "He that is without sin among you, let him first cast a stone at her," was a *greater embarrassment* to the Pharisees than his ignoring them. No stones were thrown, for *none were sinless*. They were forced to submit to *the magnificent wisdom of Jesus*. He is one of *the greatest reflections of "The Real Mind of God" that the world has ever seen*.

As for his response to the woman accused of adultery, Jesus was *afflicted by his own conscience*, as were the others who fled the scene. He was cognizant or aware of *his own sins and temptations being an imperfect human being*. This is the reason that *he rebuked even being referred to as good*. Therefore, his "neither do I condemn thee" decree was justified, indeed. Those who proclaim themselves to be Christians in this day either lack understanding or *purposely disregard* the *keywords* in verse 11 of John 8, which reveal *the stern or militant mentality* of Jesus:

"GO, AND SIN NO MORE!"

Yeah, this is the *true mentality* of Jesus that most neo-Christians *despise and purposely misrepresent*. They do not want a Jesus *with a mind of wrath, militancy, and destruction, which is the identical mentality of The Lord of the Universe, Jehovah*. No, they would rather paint a cute fantasy portrait of a *frail, fearful, timid man* who *forgives everything* or relays words similar to these:

"DO ANYTHING THAT YOU DESIRE ON EARTH,

FOR GOD FORGIVES <u>ALL</u> SINS!"

This rhetoric is *void of an atom of sanity*. No prophet of The Lord would ever relay such *idiocy (stupid statement)*. If The Lord forgives *all sins* (as most Christians *ignorantly* believe and declare), *Jeffery Dahmer, Jack the Ripper, Ted Bundy, and all other serial-killers*, are certainly sitting on heavenly thrones, sipping heavenly lattes, clothed in heavenly garments, in the presence of The Lord *in eternal paradise, for no one is sent to Hell, because* "God is Love" *and forgives all sins,* correct? Some Christians know that this *ridiculous fantasy* is certainly *an abomination to The Real Jesus*. Let us return to the woman in verse 11 of John 8. Jesus *did not ask but demanded* that she "sin no more!" The conclusion that should be drawn is that if he were to catch her in an act of adultery, *he would (personally) stone her to death.* Aye, this is the *true mentality* of The Real Jesus. There are *LIMITS to mercy or forgiveness* with The Lord of the Cosmos. Hence, any who *ignorantly or defiantly* believe that they can commit any sin that they desire (for as long as they desire) and The Lord will *repeatedly forgive* these sins, are as far away from *reality* and "The Real Mind of God" as Pluto is from the Sun. Here is further corroboration for my decree regarding the *stern, militant* Jesus:

Bible / John 5

12. Then asked they him, What man is that which said unto thee, Take up thy bed, and walk?

13. And he that was healed wist not who it was: for Jesus had conveyed himself away, a multitude being in that place.

14. Afterward Jesus findeth him in the temple, and said unto him, Behold, thou art made whole: _SIN NO MORE, lest a worse thing come unto thee_!

Yeah, Jesus _was a stern solider_ of The Lord who _issued commands, not timid - whimpering pleas_. Here are the alleged words of Jesus _regarding himself and his mission_:

Bible / Matthew 5

17. Think _NOT_ that I am come to _destroy the law, or the prophets_: I am not come to destroy, _but to fulfill_.

Consequently, _inconsistencies_ or _contradictions_ found in the decrees of Jesus (relative to previous prophets) have _purposely been inserted_ by sinister demons of Satan housed in human skin suits. Here is an example of their wicked _insertions_ into a decree of The Real Jesus:

Bible / Mark 3

28. Verily I say unto you, _ALL SINS shall be forgiven_ unto the sons of men, and blasphemies wherewith soever they shall blaspheme:

29. But he that shall blaspheme against the Holy Ghost hath _never forgiveness_, but is in danger of _eternal damnation_.

Verse 28 of Mark 3 is certainly *inconsistent* with the decrees of the prophets of The Lord prior to Jesus. Therefore, the word *"shall"* is an *evil insertion* to *incite rebellion* against the previous laws or commandments of The Lord. Inserting the word *"shall"* into the phrase, makes one believe that he or she can *commit any and every sin that they desire, for all sins will certainly (shall) be forgiven* by The Lord of the Worlds; *except cursing him* or his unseen hosts. Satan and his demonic legion *love to incite rebellion* in mankind by deceit.

There are yet and still *fragments of truth* within The Bible if the satanic hieroglyphics can be deciphered. In verse 29 of Mark 3, the "never forgiveness, but is in danger of eternal damnation" decree is *congruent or consistent* with "The Real Mind of God" from the beginning of The Bible (Genesis) to the tabloid *alleged (keyword)* Gospels of Jesus: *Matthew*, *Luke*, *Mark* and *John*. Actually, The Holy Qur'an *rectifies and ratifies* the satanic *insertion of certainty (shall)* in verse 28 of Mark 3:

Holy Qur'an / Surah 4

116. Surely Allah *forgives not setting up partners with Him*, and He forgives all besides this *to whom He pleases*. And whoever sets up a partner with Allah, he indeed goes far astray.

The "to whom he pleases" phrase in the verse *destroys the false sense of certainty* in verse 28 of Mark 3. In simpler terms, The Lord *may or might forgive your sins; not shall or will forgive your sins*. *Semantics* (the study of *meanings*) is *vital for deciphering the hieroglyphics* of The Bible, indeed. Hence, any decrees alleged to be from Jesus that *CONTRADICT* the established laws of The Lord, are satanic insertions by human demons. Here is a *monumental insertion of contradiction* that has been ascribed to *John* the disciple of Jesus:

Bible / 1 John 3

8. He that committeth *sin is of the devil*; for the devil sinneth from the beginning. For this purpose the Son of God was manifested, that he might *destroy the works* of the devil.

9. Whosoever is *born of God doth not commit sin*; for his seed remaineth in him: and *he cannot sin*, because he is *born of God*.

If John relayed the preceding precisely as you see it written, *he is a lying demon in a skin suit*. However, if John *did not* relay the preceding, *demons* in skin suits have *diabolically inserted contradictions* to destroy the complete truth from The Lord of the Universe. Using the absurd reasoning of these verses, Jesus himself was "of the devil," for *he despised even being called good, killed an innocent fig tree, transformed water into forbidden wine*, and perhaps many other sins *not written* in The Bible. Hence, Jesus was *by no means* the "Son of God," for according to John, he that is *born of God* "*cannot sin!*" Yeah, The Bible is in *colossal confusion* due to

42

the *wicked editing* of the once pure and complete truth from the prophets of The Lord.

The Holy Qur'an and the Old Testament of The Bible resoundingly proclaim that there is not, nor has there ever been, *a single sinless man or woman upon the entire Earth*:

Holy Qur'an / Surah 16

61. And if Allah were to *destroy men for their iniquity*, He would not leave therein *a single creature*, but He respites them till an appointed time. So when their doom comes, they are not able to delay (it) an hour, nor can they advance (it).

Bible / Ecclesiastes 7

20. For there is *not a just man upon earth*, that doeth good, and *sinneth not*.

Bible / 1 Kings 8

46. If they sin against thee, (for there is *no man that sinneth not*) and thou be angry with them, and deliver them to the enemy, so that they carry them away captives unto the land of the enemy, far or near.

Therefore, every single day that you breathe upon the earth *is mercy from The Lord*, and an opportunity to *make amends or atone for your sins before you die*. In light of the preceding verses, the following decree alleged to be from Jesus is *null, void, and a manifest sinister insertion* by demons in human skin suits:

21. Then came Peter to him, and said, Lord, how oft shall my brother sin against me, and I forgive him? till seven times?

22. Jesus saith unto him, I say not unto thee, Until seven times: but, *Until seventy times seven.*

This *does not make an atom of sense and defies all sanity in the Cosmos.* No prophet of *Jehovah (God or The Lord)* since the beginning of the Earth itself had delivered any decrees even remotely resembling the preceding which has been *insidiously ascribed* to Jesus. The *asinine (extremely silly)* rhetoric in verse 22 of Matthew 18, relays that *your brother may commit 490 sins against you* before you may view him as a demon in a skin suit. The *490 times of forgiveness* is completely ridiculous and could not have come from the mouth of The Real Jesus, whatsoever. Consequently, let us use some *common sense* (which most Christians seem to be *completely devoid* of) in order to ascertain if the preceding came from the *mouth of Jesus:*

1. If your brother (either your biological brother or merely someone that you view as your brother) *grabs a knife and kills your mother,* would you forgive him another 489 times?

2. If that same brother enters your house and *steals your money and other belongings,* would you forgive him another 488 times?

3. If that same brother *steals your car* and has an accident, would you forgive him another 487 times?

4. If that same brother *gives your child cocaine* resulting in your *child's addiction* to the substance, would you forgive him another 486 times?

I do not believe that I need to outline another *485 civil violations* for you to ascertain that allowing another human being (brother or other) to commit crimes or sins against you *repeatedly*, means that *you are either a complete idiot or hopelessly insane*. Hence, a man of such boundless wisdom as Jesus *would never have relayed that* "until seventy times seven" *rhetoric of insanity to anyone at any time, whatsoever.*

Another monumental falsehood perpetuated by rebellious Christians is that the *crucifixion of Jesus* (resulting in his *perceived* death) was to *cleanse or remove the sins of the entire Earth*. Here is the proclamation *alleged* to be from *John* (disciple of Jesus):

Bible / John 1

29. The next day John seeth Jesus coming unto him, and saith, Behold the Lamb of God, *which taketh away the sin of the world.*

Bible / 1 John 3

5. And ye know that he was manifested to *take away our sins*; and *in him is no sin*.

If you are of sanity, you most certainly realize that the preceding is *absolutely absurd* to say the least. Again, if John actually relayed this, *he is a lying demon in a skin suit*.

However, if this was *diabolically inserted* into the alleged words of John by *white Jews* (and others), they have obeyed the command of *their father Satan* to perfection: *"Destroy the straight path or complete truth from The Lord by any and every means necessary!"*

Since I have outlined the *sins of Jesus* in this book, you now know that verse 5 of 1 John 3 (*alleged letters* from John the Disciple) are *null and completely void of sanity*. As for verse 29 of John 1, the "taketh away the sin of the world" rhetoric is also *null and completely void of sanity* for the manifest fact that human beings across the entire Earth are *indulging in more sin in this modern day, than at any other time in history; probably since the beginning or formation of the earth itself.* Consequently, how in sanity could Jesus have *died to remove the sin of the world*, when the world in this day is *more sinful or wicked than Sodom, Gomorrah, Babylon, Egypt, Rome, and all of the other Satanic empires of mortals combined?* Therefore, Jesus could not have possibly died *to cleanse the world of sin, for he was a sinner himself and despised even being referred to as* "good" according to The Bible. Here is a reminder of this in case you have forgotten:

Bible / Luke 18

18. And a certain ruler asked him, saying, *Good Master*, what shall I do to inherit eternal life?

19. And Jesus said unto him, *Why callest thou me good? none is good, save one, that is, God.*

Aye, a sinner (Jesus) could not have possibly *died to cleanse* all of the men and women of the entire Earth from their sins, whatsoever. That is *illogical, preposterous, and insults the intelligence of all beings with functioning brain cells*; a few Christians know this. However, I understand their confusion regarding The Bible, for it is a *gargantuan jigsaw puzzle of lies mixed with fragments of truth*. Here are examples of the lies that Satan's children have inserted into the once pure truth from The Lord of the Universe:

BIBLE CONTRADICTIONS

Bible / Deuteronomy 24

16. The fathers *shall not be put to death* for the children, *neither shall the children* be put to death for the fathers: every man shall be put to death for *his own sin*.

Bible / Isaiah 14

21. Prepare *slaughter for his children for the iniquity of their fathers*; that they do not rise, nor possess the land, nor fill the face of the world with cities.

Bible / Galatians 6

2. *Bear ye one another's burdens*, and so fulfill the law of Christ.

5. For every man *shall bear his own burden*.

As you can clearly see, The Bible in this day is a *cesspool* that has been *created by Satan and his scripture editing white Jew children* (and others) as declared by Jesus himself.

Now, *only one* of the preceding contradictory verses is right and exact. Either a person *can or cannot carry another person's burden*. Either the children *can or cannot be put to death for the sins of their fathers*. Henceforth, Satan's demons have *diabolically inserted* these contradictions throughout The Bible.

In light of the manifest confusion in The Bible, *I thank The Lord (daily)* for revealing the *final scripture* upon the earth which *ratifies and rectifies* The Bible:

Holy Qur'an / Surah 53

38. That *no bearer of a burden bears another's burden*:

Holy Qur'an / Surah 35

18. And *no burdened soul can bear another's burden*. And if one weighed down by a burden calls another to carry his load, *naught of it will be carried*, even though he be *near of kin*. Thou warnest only those who fear their Lord in secret and keep up prayer. And whoever purifies himself, purifies himself *only for his own good*. And to Allah is the eventual coming.

Yeah, these verses are *supremely logical*. Jesus knew full well that his death *would not eliminate or nullify the sins of anyone, anywhere, at any time whatsoever*. Therefore, the following decrees have been *diabolically inserted* as well:

Bible / John 4

42. And said unto the woman, Now we believe, not because of thy saying: for we have heard him ourselves, and know that this is indeed *the Christ, the Saviour of the world*.

49

51. I am the living bread which came down from heaven: if any man eat of this bread, he shall live for ever: and the bread that I will give is my flesh, which *I will give for the life of the world*.

These verses are *completely absurd* as are all others like them in The Bible. *No single human being is (or was) the "savior of the world,"* period. This is *blasphemy* to say the least. Jesus delivers the criterion for discerning lies and evil from truth and righteousness, thusly:

Bible / Matthew 12

33. Either *make the tree good*, and his *fruit good*; or else *make the tree corrupt*, and his *fruit corrupt*: for the tree is *known by his fruit*.

In light of this *divine criterion*, how in sanity can Jesus be the "savior of the world," and give his life for the "life of the world," when these (in this *21st Century*) still exists: *FAMINE, MURDER, WAR, HOMOSEXUALITY, THIEVERY, PORNOGRAPHY, HOMELESSNESS, DISEASE, ATHEISM, HATRED, INFIDELITY, GAMBLING, RAPE, ALCOHOLISM, SPOUSAL ABUSE, DRUG ADDICTION, and the rest?*

In light of the preceding, if Jesus gave his life for the world or came to *save it from its sins, his death was worthless, in vain, and insignificant*. If the tree is known by its fruit, the *Tree of Jesus has produced fruit of boundless evil,* which makes his giving his life *a complete failure.*

Jesus would never have declared himself to be the *savior of the earth, remover of the sins of the earth*, nor any other completely ridiculous rhetoric such as this. All of this foolishness was *inserted into The Bible* by demons in skin suits. Here are further inserted verses of utterly asinine rhetoric:

Bible / John 3

16. For God so *loved the world,* that he *gave his only begotten Son,* that whosoever believeth in him should not perish, but have everlasting life.

17. For God *sent not* his Son into the world *to condemn the world;* but that *the world through him might be saved.*

Bible / John 12

46. I am come a light into the world, that whosoever believeth on me should not abide in darkness.

47. And if any man hear my words, and believe not, *I judge him not*: for I came *not to judge the world, but to save the world.*

These verses are also *absolutely ridiculous, and an insult to the intelligence of the sane.* Now, how in sanity could Jesus have come to *save the world, without having JUDGED that the world was sick or evil, and needed to be saved from that sickness or evil, eh?* Here are the *colossal contradictions* to the preceding verses that the demons in skin suits *did not edit*:

39. And Jesus said, *For judgment I am come into this world*, that they which see not might see; and that they which see might be made blind.

21. Then said Jesus again unto them, I go my way, and ye shall seek me, and *shall die in your sins*: whither I go, ye cannot come.

22. Then said the Jews, Will he kill himself? because he saith, Whither I go, ye cannot come.

23. And he said unto them, *Ye are from beneath*; I am from above: *ye are of this world*; I am *not of this world*.

24. I said therefore unto you, that *ye shall die in your sins*: for if ye believe not that I am he, *ye shall die in your sins*.

Perhaps, we should define the word "judge" in order to shine the *light of sanity* upon The Bible verses of contradiction:

Merriam Webster's Dictionary / JUDGE:

1: *to form an opinion* about through careful *weighing of evidence* and *testing of premises*

2 : to *sit in judgment* on : Try

3 : *to determine* or pronounce after inquiry and deliberation

4 : Govern, Rule-- used of a Hebrew tribal leader

5 : *to form an estimate or evaluation of ; especially* : to form a negative opinion about <shouldn't *judge* him because of his accent>

In light of these definitions, the "*shall* die in your sins" terminology in verse 21 of John 8, is a *resoundingly definitive declaration*, which makes it *a judgment* of Jesus. Notice that he did not tell the Jews that they *may or might* die in their sins, but that *they shall or will die in their sins*. How can this be if *his death were to cleanse or save the whole earth from sin*, eh? In the immortal words of Dr. Spock: "*Illogical*, Captain Kirk."

Every single Jew to whom Jesus was speaking would have to have *died before himself* in order to die "in their sins," for if they died *after his death*, the *sins of all upon the entire earth are erased or eliminated completely*. Again, demons in skin suits merely *concocted and inserted* the "Savior of the world, judge not the world, dying for the sins of the world," and the rest of that preposterous rhetoric into The Bible. In fact, Jesus was *so enraged and disgusted with this physical world*, he relayed this to The Lord of the Cosmos:

Bible / John 17

6. I have manifested thy name unto the men which thou gavest me out of the world: thine they were, and thou gavest them me; and they have kept thy word.

53

7. Now they have known that all things whatsoever thou hast given me are of thee.

8. For I have given unto them the words which thou gavest me; and they have received them, and have known surely that I came out from thee, and they have believed that thou didst send me.

9. *I pray for them: I PRAY NOT FOR THE WORLD*, but for them which thou hast given me; for they are thine.

Consequently, how in sanity can a man (Jesus) who *refuses to offer even a single prayer for this wretched world*, be the *savior, cleanser, or martyr for it*, eh? This does not make *an atom of sense to any being with a single functioning brain cell*. Don't you think that *offering a mere prayer* for the world is far easier than *giving your life for it?*

Well, let us further explore the true *militant-annihilator mentality* of Jesus that is *hated by most fantasy-loving Christians:*

Bible / Matthew 18

6. But whoso shall offend one of these little ones which believe in me, it were better for him that a *millstone were hanged about his neck*, and that he were *drowned in the depth of the sea*.

7. *WOE UNTO THE WORLD BECAUSE OF OFFENCES!* for it must needs be that offences come; but *woe to that man by whom the offence cometh!*

Bible / Matthew 13

37. He answered and said unto them, He that soweth the good seed is the Son of man;

38. *The field is the world*; the good seed are the children of the kingdom; but *the tares are the children of the wicked one*;

39. The enemy that sowed them *is the devil*; the harvest *is the end of the world*; and the *reapers are the angels*.

40. As therefore *the tares are gathered and burned in the fire*; so shall it be in *the end of this world*.

41. The Son of man shall send forth his angels, and they shall gather out of his kingdom *all things that offend*, and *them which do iniquity*;

42. And shall *cast them into a furnace of fire*: there shall be *wailing and gnashing of teeth*.

43. Then shall the righteous shine forth as the sun in the kingdom of their Father. *Who hath ears to hear, let him hear*.

Yeah, if you have ears, *you had best hear the voice of The Real Jesus*, who was the living embodiment of *the wrath of Almighty Jehovah* (God); The Creator and Destroyer of all in the Cosmos. The preceding references (*wailing, gnashing of teeth, furnace of fire, tares, the end of the world, millstone around the neck, drowning in the sea, and so on*) are *not in accord* with the proper speech of one who had allegedly *come to save the world*, whatsoever. Therefore, *any contradictions* to the preceding declarations from *The Real Jesus* have been *inserted by demons* in skin suits. Here are further declarations from Jesus that are *parallel in nature* to those of the prophets before him:

Bible / Matthew 24

21. For then shall be *great tribulation*, such as was not *since the beginning of the world* to this time, no, *nor ever shall be*.
22. And except those days should be shortened, *there should no flesh be saved*: but for the elect's sake those days shall be shortened.

Bible / Matthew 18

8. Wherefore if thy hand or thy foot offend thee, *cut them off*, and cast them from thee: it is better for thee to enter into life *halt or maimed*, rather than having two hands or two feet to be *cast into everlasting fire*.
9. And if thine eye offend thee, *pluck it out*, and cast it from thee: it is better for thee to *enter into life with one eye*, rather than having two eyes to be *cast into hell fire*.

What? *Great tribulation? Cut off your hand or your foot? Pluck out your eye? Cast into hell fire?* This line of speech is certainly *not indicative of a man who came to save the world nor die for it*, whatsoever. This line of speech is a manifestation of *a mentality of wrath and punishment*. In light of these decrees from *The Real Jesus*, how in sanity can alleged Christians believe that *Jesus forgives all sins and loves everyone*, when this man clearly advocated CASTING THE WICKED

INTO HELL? Most Christians are in a *perpetual state of delusion and confusion* regarding *The Real* Jesus.

Let us now hear the alleged voice of Jesus regarding *his mission and himself*, which are as far away from dying to save this world as Pluto is from the Sun:

THE MISSION OF JESUS

Bible / Matthew 10

34. *Think NOT that I am come to send peace on earth: I came NOT to send peace, but a sword*!

35. For I am come to *set a man at variance against his father*, and *the daughter against her mother*, and the daughter in law against her mother in law.

36. And *a man's foes shall be they of his own household*.

37. He that *loveth father or mother more than me is not worthy of me*: and he that *loveth son or daughter more than me is not worthy of me*.

38. And he that taketh not his cross, and *followeth after me*, *is not worthy of me*.

Yeah, Jesus *definitively declares* that he *did not come to deliver peace to the world, save the world, remove sin from the world*, nor any of the other *pleasant bumper-sticker slogans* that alleged Christians love to relay in this day. According to these verses, Jesus was a *ferocious soldier* of The Lord who came to *separate or divide* the devout believers from the hypocrites and disbelievers.

The preceding verses are substantiated by the *abominable state of all nations* upon the Earth as I have previously mentioned. In verse 36 of Matthew 10, the "man's foes shall be they of his own household" phrase was a *prediction of the modern "Generation X"* as they have been labeled by some in the USA. The children of the USA (and around the globe) have become *vicious gang-banging murderers who are fearlessly rising against their parents*, which makes them the *enemies of their parent's households*. Consequently, Jesus' prophesy in these verses has been *resoundingly fulfilled*.

THE COMFORTER REVEALED

Most Christians are *ignorant* as to the *identity* of the one Jesus prophesied to come *after his departure*. Jesus referred to this being as the "Comforter" (or Counselor) in The Bible:

Bible / John 16

7. Nevertheless I tell you the truth; It is expedient for you that I go away: for if I go not away, *the Comforter will not come unto you*; but if I depart, *I will send him* unto you.

8. And when *he is come, he will reprove the world of sin*, and of righteousness, and of judgment:

9. Of sin, because they believe not on me;

10. Of righteousness, because I go to my Father, and *ye see me no more*;

11. Of judgment, because *the prince of this world is judged*.

In verse 8 of John 16, Jesus precisely decrees that the one coming after his departure is the "Comforter," and this being will *reprove or convict* the entire planet of sin. Consequently, this is clear evidence that Jesus was *not born to save this world nor die for it*, whatsoever. These notions are merely *juvenile fantasies that Christians have concocted in rebellion* against the actual declarations of The Real Jesus. Further, Jesus relays that *he will send another being* unto the region (Middle East) in which he lived. Jesus *did not say* that he would *send himself back to the world* to reprove it of sin, but that he would *send another being* for this purpose. This being (*The Comforter*) is none other than the *ARCH-ANGEL GABRIEL*; the most powerful and highest-ranking angel created by The Lord of the Heavens.

In verse 10 of John 16, Jesus resoundingly and definitively states that he will go to his father (*Jehovah, Allah, God, Lord, etc.*) and *will never be seen again*. Yeah, this is the complete truth, for Jesus has been *physically dead for some 2,000 years*. Therefore, Christians should stop preaching that Jesus is *returning to this physical world*; this is utter fantasy.

LUCIFER (SATAN) THE RULER OF EARTH

In verse 11 of John 16, Jesus states that "the prince of this world is judged." The "prince" terminology is a *symbolic reference to Satan* and his *absolute dominion* upon the earth by The Lord's permission:

Holy Qur'an / Surah 7

11. And We indeed created you, then We fashioned you, then We said to the angels: Make submission to Adam. So they submitted, except *Iblis; he was not of those who submitted.*

12. He (Allah) said: What hindered thee that thou didst not submit when I commanded thee? He said: *I am better than he;* Thou hast *created me of fire,* while him Thou didst *create of dust.*

13. He (Allah) said: Then get forth from this (state), for it is not for thee to behave proudly therein. Go forth, therefore, surely *thou art of the abject ones.*

14. He (Satan) said: *Respite me till the day when they are raised.*

15. He (Allah) said: Thou art surely of *the respited ones.*

16. He (Satan) said: As Thou hast adjudged me to be erring, I will certainly *lie in wait for them in Thy straight path*,

17. Then I shall certainly *come upon them from before them* and *from behind them*, and from *their right and from their left*; and Thou wilt not find *most of them thankful*.

18. He said: *Get out of it, despised*, driven away. Whoever of them will follow thee, *I will certainly fill hell with you all!*

Bible / Revelation 12

12. Therefore rejoice, ye heavens, and ye that dwell in them. *Woe to the inhabiters of the earth and of the sea! for the devil is come down unto you, having great wrath*, because he knoweth that he hath *but a short time*.

Bible / Job 1

6. Now there was a day when the sons of God came to present themselves before The Lord, and *Satan came also among them*.

7. And The Lord said unto Satan, Whence comest thou? Then Satan answered The Lord, and said, *From going to and fro in the earth, and from walking up and down in it*.

As is clear in these verses, the "prince" of the Earth is none other than *the fallen angel* of many names: *Satan, Lucifer, Mephistopheles, Mephisto, The Devil, Angra Mainyu, Mara, Diabolos, Shaitan, Ahriman, The Dragon, The Old Serpent, Loki, Set, The Beast, Baphomet*, and many other names in many different languages.

Verses 16 and 17 of Surah 7 in The Holy Qur'an, bring to mind these decrees or judgments of Jesus regarding Satan (and his demons) coming in The Lord's *straight path posing as holy men of God*:

Bible / Matthew 7

15. Beware of *false prophets*, which come to you *in sheep's clothing*, but *inwardly they are ravening wolves*.

16. Ye shall *know them by their fruits*. Do men gather grapes of thorns, or figs of thistles?

Bible / Matthew 23

1. Then spake Jesus to the multitude, and to his disciples,

2. Saying The scribes and the Pharisees sit in Moses' seat:

3. All therefore whatsoever they bid you observe, that observe and do; but *do not ye after their works: for they say, and do not.*

4. For they bind heavy burdens and grievous to be borne, and lay them on men's shoulders; but *they themselves will not move them* with one of their fingers.

5. But all their works they do for *to be seen of men*: they make broad their phylacteries, and enlarge the borders of their garments,

6. And *love the uppermost rooms* at feasts, and the *chief seats* in the synagogues,

7. And greetings in the markets, and *to be called of men, Rabbi, Rabbi*.

13. But *woe unto you*, scribes and Pharisees, *hypocrites*! for ye shut up the kingdom of heaven against men: for ye neither go in yourselves, neither suffer ye them that are entering to go in.

14. *Woe unto you*, scribes and Pharisees, *hypocrites! for ye devour widows' houses, and for a pretence make long prayer*: therefore ye shall receive *the greater damnation*.

15. *Woe unto you*, scribes and Pharisees, *hypocrites*! for ye compass sea and land to make one proselyte, and when he is made, ye make him twofold *more the child of hell than yourselves*.

24. *Ye blind guides, which strain at a gnat, and swallow a camel*.

25. *Woe unto you*, scribes and Pharisees, *hypocrites*! for ye *make clean the outside* of the cup and of the platter, but *within they are full of extortion and excess*.

26. Thou blind Pharisee, *cleanse first that which is within* the cup and platter, that the outside of them may be clean also.

27. *Woe unto you*, scribes and Pharisees, *hypocrites*! for ye are like unto *whited sepulchres*, which indeed *appear beautiful outward*, but are *within full of dead men's bones, and of all uncleanness*.

28. Even so ye also *outwardly appear righteous unto men*, but *within ye are full of hypocrisy and iniquity*.

29. *Woe unto you*, scribes and Pharisees, *hypocrites!* because ye build the tombs of the prophets, and garnish the sepulchres of the righteous,

33. *Ye serpents, ye generation of vipers, how can ye escape the damnation of hell?*

What? *A generation of vipers? Damnation of hell? Hypocrites? Ravening wolves? Child of hell? Extortion? Dead men's bones?* Now, let us be *logical* or simply use some *common sense*. Are the preceding *indictments or judgments* from Jesus in accord with those of a man who: *loves his enemies, blesses those that curse him, turns the other cheek, forgives all sins, dies to cleanse the world of sin,* and the rest of that rhetoric of insanity? No, indeed. A man relaying such slogans would be *a tremendous asset to the Roman Empire*. Caesar might even summon Jesus to be an opening speaker for his events. However, the speech in the preceding verses is in *blatant contradiction* to such slogans, and a *major factor in the crucifixion of Jesus* by the Roman and Jew demons in skin suits:

THE END OF DAYS

Bible / Matthew 24

1. And Jesus went out, and departed from the temple: and his disciples came to him for to shew him the buildings of the temple.

2. And Jesus said unto them, See ye not all these things? verily I say unto you, *There shall not be left here one stone upon another, that shall not be thrown down.*

3. And as he sat upon the mount of Olives, the disciples came unto him privately, saying, Tell us, when shall these things be? and what shall be the sign of thy coming, and of the end of the world?

4. And Jesus answered and said unto them, Take heed that no man deceive you.

5. For many *shall come in my name*, saying, I am Christ; and shall *deceive many*.

6. And ye shall hear of *wars and rumours of wars*: see that ye be not troubled: for all these things *must come to pass*, but the end is not yet.

7. *For nation shall rise against nation*, and kingdom against kingdom: and there shall be *famines, and pestilences, and earthquakes, in divers places.*

8. All these are *the beginning of sorrows.*

9. Then shall they deliver you up to be afflicted, and *shall kill you*: and ye shall be *hated of all nations* for my name's sake.

10. And then shall *many be offended, and shall betray one another, and shall hate one another.*

11. And *many false prophets shall rise, and shall deceive many.*

12. And because *iniquity shall abound*, the love of many *shall wax cold.*

13. But he that shall endure unto the end, the same shall be saved.

14. And this gospel of the kingdom shall be preached in all the world for a witness unto all nations; and *then shall the end come.*

15. When ye therefore shall see *the abomination of desolation*, spoken of by Daniel the prophet, *stand in the holy place*, (whoso readeth, let him understand:)

16. Then let them which be in Judaea flee into the mountains:

17. Let him which is on the housetop not come down to take any thing out of his house:

18. Neither let him which is in the field return back to take his clothes.

19. And *woe unto them that are with child*, and to them that give suck in those days!

20. But pray ye that your flight be not in the winter, neither on the sabbath day:

21. For then *shall be great tribulation, such as was not since the beginning of the world to this time, no, nor ever shall be.*

22. And except those days should be shortened, there should *no flesh be saved*: but for the elect's sake those days shall be shortened.

23. Then if any man shall say unto you, Lo, here is Christ, or there; *believe it not.*

24. For there shall *arise false Christs, and false prophets, and shall shew great signs and wonders*; insomuch that, if it were possible, they shall *deceive the very elect.*

25. Behold, I have told you before.

26. Wherefore if they shall say unto you, Behold, he is in the desert; go not forth: behold, he is in the secret chambers; believe it not.

27. For *as the lightning cometh out of the east, and shineth even unto the west;* so shall also the coming of the Son of man be.

28. For wheresoever the carcase is, there will the eagles be gathered together.

29. Immediately after the tribulation of those days shall *the sun be darkened, and the moon shall not give her light,* and the stars shall fall from heaven, and the powers of the heavens shall be shaken:

30. And then shall appear *the sign of the Son of man* in heaven: and then shall *all the tribes of the earth mourn,* and they shall see *the Son of man coming in the clouds of heaven with power* and great glory.

31. And *he shall send his angels* with a great sound of a trumpet, and they shall gather together his elect from the four winds, from one end of heaven to the other.

32. Now learn a parable of the fig tree; When his branch is yet tender, and putteth forth leaves, ye know that summer is nigh:

33. So likewise ye, when ye shall see all these things, know that it is near, even at the doors.

34. Verily I say unto you, This generation shall not pass, till all these things be fulfilled.

35. *Heaven and earth shall pass away,* but my words shall not pass away.

36. But of that *day and hour knoweth no man*, no, not the angels of heaven, but my Father only.

37. But as the days of Noah were, so shall also the coming of the Son of man be.

38. For as in the *days that were before the flood they were eating and drinking, marrying and giving in marriage*, until the day that Noe entered into the ark,

39. And *knew not until the flood came, and took them all away;* so shall also the coming of the Son of man be.

40. Then shall two be in the field; the *one shall be taken*, and the other left.

41. Two women shall be grinding at the mill; *the one shall be taken*, and the other left.

42. Watch therefore: for *ye know not what hour* your Lord doth come.

43. But know this, that if the good man of the house had known in what watch the thief would come, he would have watched, and would not have suffered his house to be broken up.

44. Therefore be ye also ready: for *in such an hour as ye think not* the Son of man cometh.

45. Who then is a faithful and wise servant, whom his lord hath made ruler over his household, to give them meat in due season?

46. Blessed is that servant, whom his lord when he cometh shall find so doing.

47. Verily I say unto you, That he shall make him ruler over all his goods.

48. But and if that evil servant shall say in his heart, My lord delayeth his coming;

49. And shall begin to *smite his fellow servants*, and to eat and *drink with the drunken*;

50. The Lord of that servant shall come in a day when he looketh not for him, and in an hour that he is not aware of,

51. And shall *cut him asunder*, and appoint him *his portion with the hypocrites: there shall be weeping and gnashing of teeth!*

As is clear from this entire chapter, Christians who continue to rebelliously proclaim that *Jesus died to save the world*, are as far away from the complete truth as Pluto is from the Sun.

In verse 15 of Matthew 24, Jesus prophesied of the "abomination of desolation" standing in the holy place. This abomination that produces desolation is *The USSA (United Satanic States of America) whose military stood in the holy city of Mecca, Arabia in this current millennium*. The white race of the USSA is the only race to have actually *unleashed their nuclear abomination weapons* upon the cities of *Hiroshima* and *Nagasaki* in Japan. On August 6, 1945, the USSA dropped an *atom bomb* on Hiroshima. Three days later, another atom bomb was dropped on Nagasaki. The estimated death toll from the two bombings is *well over one-quarter of a million (250,000) human beings.* To this very day, the soil in both cities *remains radioactive,* and Japanese children currently suffer from *birth deformities* as a result of the *atomic energy* that was unleashed in 1945 by the alleged *good ole Jesus-loving Christians of the USSA;* so much for Jesus giving his life to save the world, eh?

In verse 27 of Matthew 24, Jesus *symbolically* declares that a "lightning" will come out of the East that will shine bright enough to be *seen in the West (USSA).* This prophesy is of the *nuclear bomb* that will *inevitably be unleashed in the lands of the Middle East.* Jesus was ever cunning in his use of symbolism. Even if those in the USSA could not literally see the nuclear explosion and mushroom cloud, the *entire planet would suffer the effects of the "abomination of desolation"* for millenniums to come.

In verse 29 of Matthew 24, Jesus proclaims that after the "abomination of desolation" *(mass-global destruction weapons)* is unleashed in the holy lands of the East: "the Sun will be darkened, the Moon shall not give her light, the Stars will fall, and the Heavens will be shaken."

Again, let us venture into the realm of *common sense.* Now, if Jesus offered to *give his life (die on the cross) to save the world,* why in sanity *would he predict the future annihilation of that same world,* eh? Does this make *an atom of sense* to you? I think not. Yeah, that divine soldier named Jesus was speaking of the *radioactive fallout* that would occur after the "abomination of desolation" was unleashed. A modern nuclear bomb (if dropped upon the surface of the Earth) would explode and produce heat temperatures of *over 50,000,000 (fifty million) degrees centigrade*. This unimaginable heat would *vaporize all animate and inanimate objects*. The dirt and debris hurled into the atmosphere would be *radioactive*, which is referred to as "radioactive fallout." Hence, the "lightening" and the "shaken" heavens that Jesus refers to is the *nuclear explosion itself*. The "darkened" Sun and Moon is the *radioactive dirt and debris*, which produces the *mushroom cloud* that will *cover the sky and eclipse the Sun* for a time. Some scientists claim that if a number of nuclear warheads were dropped upon the surface of the earth, the smoke and debris would *blanket the sky and produce a "nuclear winter."* In other words, the Sun would not be able to *penetrate the smoke and debris within our atmosphere for years*.

If you are of those who possess *common sense*, you know that all life upon the Earth (human and other) would *cease to exist without the Sun*. Only a *race of demons in skin suits* would make such weapons of *global destruction*, correct? I will let Jesus relay his answer to this question:

Bible / John 8

44. _YE ARE OF YOUR FATHER THE DEVIL_, and the lusts of your father ye will do. He was _A MURDERER FROM THE BEGINNING_, and abode _not in the truth_, because there is _no truth in him_. When he speaketh _a lie_, he speaketh _of his own: for he is a liar, and the father of it._

I am in _complete agreement_ with his assessment of _the white race; they love to lie and murder for sport_, indeed. Verses 37-39 of Matthew 24 is another prophesy of Jesus which has actually been fulfilled in this day. In these verses, Jesus declares that a _great flood shall come and wash human beings away,_ as was the case with those who did not follow Noah into the Ark within The Bible. Jesus relayed that humans would be "eating, drinking, and marrying" until a great flood destroyed all of them. Well, this was manifest in the _Indian Ocean Earthquake of December 2004, and subsequent tsunamis of epic proportions_. This earthquake is alleged to have been _9.3 in magnitude_, which is said to be the _second largest in recorded history_. The _tsunamis_ (Jesus says: "Great Flood") that followed this quake are said to have claimed the lives of some _250,000 men, women, and babies, while they were eating, drinking, and marrying_ as Jesus predicted. Henceforth, these declarations are as far away from a man _giving his life to save the world_ as Pluto is from the Sun. Let us now return to the _indignant and militant mentality_ of Jesus that alleged Christians _despise_:

THE CALLOUS JESUS

Bible / Matthew 8

19. And a certain scribe came, and said unto him, Master, I will follow thee whithersoever thou goest.

20. And Jesus saith unto him, The foxes have holes, and the birds of the air have nests; but the *Son of man hath not where to lay his head*.

21. And another of his disciples said unto him, Lord, suffer me first to go and bury my father.

22. But Jesus said unto him, Follow me; and *let the dead bury their dead*.

Bible / Luke 9

61. And another also said, Lord, I will follow thee; *but let me first go bid them farewell*, which are at home at my house.

62. And Jesus said unto him, No man, having put his hand to the plough, and *looking back, is fit for the kingdom of God*.

What? The dead father of this individual is *irrelevant*, so "let the dead bury their dead?" Those in the home of the other individual are also *irrelevant*, so telling them farewell makes this individual "unfit" for the Kingdom of God? Isn't it strange that you don't find verses such as these on the *car bumper-stickers of alleged Christians?* This is because they *love their preferred fantasy Jesus*, rather than *the real one* in these verses:

Bible / Luke 19

27. But those *mine enemies*, which would not that I should reign over them, bring hither, and <u>SLAY them before me</u>.

What? Jesus demands that *his enemies be killed in front of him?* Yeah, this is *The Real Mind of Jesus* that is in perfect accord with the *prophets before him* and "The Real Mind of God:"

Bible / Luke 22

35. And he said unto them, When I sent you without purse, and scrip, and shoes, lacked ye any thing? And they said, Nothing.

36. Then said he unto them, *But now*, he that hath a purse, let him take it, and likewise his scrip: and <u>he that hath no sword, let him sell his garment, and buy one</u>.

37. For I say unto you, that this that is written must yet be accomplished in me, And he was reckoned among the transgressors: for the things concerning me have an end.

38. And they said, Lord, behold, *here are two swords*. And he said unto them, *It is enough*.

What? Jesus *commands his disciples to buy swords?* They should even *sell their own clothes to buy these swords?* Do you think that these swords are for *a giant shish-kebab or for battle?* Yeah, this is the *militant, merciless-Jesus* that Christians *do not like nor want.* They prefer a *whimpering little punk-Jesus* who loves everyone and forgives everything; a convenient little *fantasy for adult-infants,* indeed:

Bible / Matthew 12

46. While he yet talked to the people, behold, *his mother* and his brethren stood without, *desiring to speak with him.*

47. Then one said unto him, Behold, thy mother and thy brethren stand without, desiring to speak with thee.

48. But he answered and said unto him that told him, *Who is my mother? and who are my brethren?*

49. And he stretched forth his hand toward *his disciples,* and said, *Behold my mother and my brethren!*

50. For whosoever shall do the will of my Father which is in heaven, *the same is my brother, and sister, and mother.*

The actual stepbrothers of Jesus (*James, Joses, Simon, and Judas*) are referred to in verse 46 of Matthew 12 as "brethren." Consequently, I can understand Jesus making his stepbrothers wait until his sermon was complete before addressing them. However, I do not believe that Jesus (as stern as he was) would *disrespect his mother (Mary) in such fashion* as to make her wait

78

to speak to him. Especially, since Mary was a *devout believing servant* of The Lord of the Worlds. Hence, the preceding verses have been *diabolically edited* by demons in skin suits. In fact, The Holy Qur'an declares this regarding the *Mother of Jesus*:

Holy Qur'an / Surah 3

42. And when the angels said: *O Mary*, surely Allah has *chosen thee and purified thee* and chosen thee *above the women of the world*.

43. *O Mary*, be obedient to thy Lord and humble thyself and bow down with those who bow.

In light of these decrees, Jesus *would not dare disrespect his mother (Mary) in any fashion, whatsoever*. Here are a few other *satanic additions and distortions* in The Bible:

Bible / John 2

1. And the third day there was a marriage in Cana of Galilee; and the mother of Jesus was there:

2. And both Jesus was called, and his disciples, to the marriage.

3. And when they wanted wine, *the mother of Jesus saith unto him, They have no wine*.

4. Jesus saith unto her, *Woman, what have I to do with thee?* mine hour is not yet come.

Well, I do not know about you, but if I were to refer to my mother as "woman" (or even use *her first name*), she would have *slapped my face off*. Again, I do not believe that Jesus would have addressed his divine mother in such a *disrespectful manner*, whatsoever. Further, I do not believe that Mary would encourage Jesus to *make wine which is disliked by The Lord* of the Heavens; these acts have been *inserted* into The Bible by demons.

Bible / John 19

25. Now there stood by the cross of Jesus his mother, and his mother's sister, Mary the wife of Cleophas, and *Mary Magdalene*.

26. When Jesus therefore saw his mother, and *the disciple standing by, whom he loved*, he saith unto his mother, *Woman, behold thy son!*

27. Then saith he to *the disciple, Behold thy mother!* And from that hour *that disciple* took her unto *his* own home.

DISCIPLE WHOM JESUS LOVED

Again, we have Jesus allegedly addressing his *divine mother (Mary)* as "woman." Further, this mysterious "disciple whom Jesus loved" is none other than his *stepbrother JAMES*:

Bible / Galatians 1

19. But other of the apostles saw I none, save *James The Lord's brother*.

Bible / 1 Corinthians 15

7. After that, he was *seen of James*; then of all the apostles.

Bible / Acts 12

16. But *Peter* continued knocking: and when they had opened the door, and saw him, they were astonished.

17. But he, beckoning unto them with the hand to hold their peace, declared unto them how The Lord had brought him out of the prison. And he said, Go *shew these things unto James*, and to the brethren. And he departed, and went into another place.

Bible Acts 21

18. And the day following *Paul* went in with us *unto James;* and all the elders were present.

It is clear in these verses that *James was so highly regarded by Jesus,* even *Peter* (and other disciples) desired that *James be made aware of important affairs.* Jesus *loved or favored* his *stepbrother James,* indeed.

Jesus also loved another disciple of his who was *present at the site of his crucifixion, his wife Mary Magdalene.* Hence, verse 27 of John 19, is a *partial truth* that has been *edited by women-hating* demons in skin suits. Those who hide and guard the ancient scrolls that comprise The Bible *did not want the world to know that Jesus had a spouse, and that she was his disciple in addition to his twelve male disciples.* Yeah, the complete truth is being revealed in these last days, indeed. I will continue this subject latter. Let us again return to the *indignant, militant mentality* of The Real Jesus that alleged Christians *despise.*

PONTIUS PILATE & KING HEROD

Bible / John 19

7. The Jews answered him, We have a law, and by our law he ought to die, because he made himself the Son of God.

8. When Pilate therefore heard that saying, he was the more afraid;

9. And went again into the judgment hall, and saith unto Jesus, *Whence art thou? But Jesus gave him no answer.*

10. Then saith Pilate unto him, Speakest thou not unto me? knowest thou not that I have power to crucify thee, and have power to release thee?

Bible / Matthew 26

61. And said, This fellow said, I am able to destroy the temple of God, and to build it in three days.

62. And the high priest arose, and said unto him, *Answerest thou nothing?* what is it which these witness against thee?

63. *But Jesus held his peace*, And the high priest answered and said unto him, I adjure thee by the living God, that thou tell us whether thou be the Christ, the Son of God.

Bible / Luke 23

8. And when Herod saw Jesus, he was exceeding glad: for he was desirous to see him of a long season, because he had heard many things of him; and he hoped to have seen some miracle done by him.

9. Then he questioned with him in many words; *but he answered him nothing*.

10. And the chief priests and scribes stood and vehemently accused him.

What kind of man must Jesus have been to *ignore and defy not only the King of the Jews (Herod) himself, but also a ranking governor (Pontius Pilate) and the military guards of one of the most brutally savage regimes (Roman Empire) in the history of human existence?* Could he have been the *timid little "love thy enemies" wimp* of Christian fantasy, or an *indignant fearless warrior* for The Lord of the Worlds? I conclude the latter to be *the complete truth*. Let us continue with the interrogation of this divine soldier of The Lord:

Bible / Mark 15

2. And Pilate asked him, *Art thou the King of the Jews?* And he answering said unto them, *Thou sayest it*.

3. And the chief priests accused him of many things: *but he answered nothing.*

4. And Pilate asked him again, saying, *Answerest thou nothing?* behold how many things they witness against thee.

5. *But Jesus yet answered nothing;* so that *Pilate marvelled.*

In verse 2 of Mark 15, Jesus elevates his *blatant defiance and disdain* by breaking his silence with the 16th century English equivalent of what many in this modern day say when thoroughly *irritated* with someone: "*Kiss my behind!*" Yeah, the "thou sayest it" answer regarding his being the "King of the Jews" is *absolutely hilarious.* In current English, Jesus simply said to Pilate: "*I never told a single person that I was the King of the Jews; so why in hell are you asking me this stupid question?*" Yeah, Jesus was ever *cunning and indignant* with his enemies, indeed. He raises his level of *sarcasm and defiance* even higher in the following:

Bible / John 18

19. The high priest then asked Jesus of his disciples, and of his doctrine.

20. Jesus answered him, *I spake openly to the world;* I ever taught in the synagogue, and in the temple, whither the Jews always resort; and *in secret have I said nothing.*

21. *Why askest thou me? ask them which heard me,* what I have said unto them: behold, *they know what I said.*

22. And when he had thus spoken, one of the officers which stood by *struck Jesus* with the palm of his hand, saying, Answerest thou the high priest so?

23. Jesus answered him, If I have spoken evil, *bear witness of the evil*: but if well, *why smitest thou me?*

Again, in verse 21 of John 18, we find Jesus saying the 16th century English equivalent of *"kiss my behind!"* In current English, Jesus said the following: *"Dude, you are getting on my nerves and I'm tired of talking to you. All of you human demons know my charges against you. So, hurry up and crucify me, then go to hell."*

In verse 22, the officer was so enraged by the *sarcasm* of Jesus, he hit him. Jesus responds in his typical *fearless soldier fashion* with the "bear witness of the evil" challenge to the buffoon. Yeah, Jesus was ever *cunning and indignant* with his enemies indeed:

Bible / John 18

33. Then Pilate entered into the judgment hall again, and called Jesus, and said unto him, *Art thou the King of the Jews?*

34. Jesus answered him, *Sayest thou this thing of thyself*, or did *others tell it thee of me?*

35. Pilate answered, Am I a Jew? Thine *own nation* and the *chief priests have delivered thee* unto me: what hast thou done?

36. Jesus answered, My kingdom is not of this world: if my kingdom were of this world, *then would my servants fight*, that I should *not be delivered to the Jews*: but now is my kingdom not from hence.

37. Pilate therefore said unto him, *Art thou a king then?* Jesus answered, *Thou sayest that I am a king*. To this end was I born, and for this cause came I into the world, that *I should bear witness unto the truth*. Every one that is of the truth *heareth my voice*.

Yet again, we have Jesus responding in the fashion of a *fearless soldier, not a whimpering punk*. Further, there was Jew outrage around the world regarding actor-director Mel Gibson's "Passion of the Christ" film. However, as is clear in verses 35 and 36 of John 18, the *real death squad or attempted murderers of Jesus were the white Jew demons in skin suits*. Regardless of how much *they hate* being referred to as *the (attempted) murderers* of Jesus, *they were the culprits*. Here is further evidence of the *Jews savagely screaming for the murder of Jesus*:

Bible / Matthew 27

20. But the chief priests and elders *persuaded* the multitude that they should *ask Barabbas, and destroy Jesus*.

21. The governor answered and said unto them, Whether of the twain will ye that I release unto you? *They said, Barabbas*.

22. Pilate saith unto them, What shall I do then with Jesus which is called Christ? *They all say unto him, Let him be crucified.*

23. And the *governor* said, *Why, what evil hath he done?* But *they cried out the more, saying, Let him be crucified.*

24. When *Pilate saw that he could prevail nothing*, but that rather a tumult was made, he *took water, and washed his hands before the multitude*, saying, *I AM INNOCENT of the blood of this just person: SEE YE TO IT.*

25. Then answered *all the people*, and said, *HIS BLOOD BE ON US, and on OUR CHILDREN!*

26. Then released he Barabbas unto them: and when he had scourged Jesus, he delivered him to be crucified.

Again, the Jews were the *de facto murderers of Jesus* no matter how much they despise being referred to in such manner. *His blood is on their hands* as verse 25 of Matthew 27, resoundingly and definitively states. For the final time, let us return to the *militant* Jesus:

Bible / Matthew 4

1. Then was Jesus led up of the Spirit into the wilderness to be tempted of the devil.

2. And when he had fasted forty days and forty nights, he was afterward an hungred.

3. And when the tempter came to him, he said, If thou be the Son of God, *command that these stones be made bread.*

4. But he answered and said, It is written, Man shall not live *by bread alone, but by every word* that proceedeth out of the mouth of God.

5. Then the devil taketh him up into the holy city, and setteth him on a pinnacle of the temple,

6. And saith unto him, If thou be the Son of God, *cast thyself down*: for it is written, He shall give his angels charge concerning thee: and in their hands they shall bear thee up, lest at any time thou dash thy foot against a stone.

7. Jesus said unto him, It is written again, *Thou shalt not tempt The Lord thy God.*

8. Again, the devil taketh him up into an exceeding high mountain, and sheweth him *all the kingdoms of the world,* and the glory of them;

9. And saith unto him, All these things *will I give thee,* if thou wilt *fall down and worship me.*

10. Then saith Jesus unto him, *Get thee hence, Satan*: for it is written, Thou shalt *worship The Lord thy God, and him only* shalt thou serve.

11. Then *the devil leaveth him,* and, behold, angels came and ministered unto him.

Jesus was *indignant and defiant even unto Satan himself.*
Alleged Christians are fond of their ("love thy enemies")
fantasy Jesus. Amusingly however, whenever I confront them with
this simple question:

"Does Jesus love Satan?"

Most often, rather than relay the correct response *(Jesus DOES
NOT love Satan)*, they either *change the subject completely*, or
excuse themselves from my presence. Hence, alleged Christians
are as far away from *The Real Jesus* as Pluto is from the Sun.

Let us now address this "Son of God" business which
Christians have either *completely misunderstood* or *purposely
misrepresented* to the masses:.

THE SONS OF GOD

Bible / Luke 3

38. Which was the son of Enos, which was the son of Seth, which was the *son of Adam*, which was the <u>*SON OF GOD*</u>.

Once again, let us use a bit of *common sense*. Since the preceding verse definitively declares that *Adam was the "Son of God,"* this delivers *the fatal blow to Christianity*. Since, *Adam was the first and only human being* made or created from *dust, dirt, mud, or clay* (whichever you prefer) by The Lord of the Worlds, *then Adam (NOT JESUS) is the only human male that could actually be hailed as the "Son of God."* Aye, Jesus was made *within the womb of a woman* as are all other human beings; *ADAM WAS NOT.* Consequently, Jesus was no more the "Son of God" than *any other human males (except Adam)* past or present, whatsoever. The Holy Qur'an addresses the issue as follows:

Holy Qur'an / Surah 3

59. The likeness of *Jesus* with Allah is truly as the likeness of *Adam. He created him from dust, then said to him, Be, and he was.*

60. (This is) *the truth* from thy Lord, so be not of the disputers.

61. Whoever then disputes with thee in this matter after the knowledge that has come to thee, say: Come! Let us call our sons and your sons and our women and your women and our people and your people, then let us be earnest in prayer, and *invoke the curse of Allah on the liars.*

62. Surely this is the *true account,* and there is no god but Allah, and Allah, he surely is the Mighty, the Wise.

Further, Jesus delivers the *reason and definition (proper context)* for his use of the "Son of God" terminology:

Bible / John 10

30. I and my Father *are one.*

31. Then the Jews took up stones again to stone him.

32. Jesus answered them, Many good works have I shewed you *from my Father;* for which of those works do ye stone me?

33. The Jews answered him, saying, For a good work we stone thee not; but for blasphemy; and because that thou, being a man, *makest thyself God.*

34. Jesus answered them, Is it not *written in your law,* I said, *Ye are gods?*

35. If *he called them gods*, unto whom the word of God came, and the scripture cannot be broken;

36. Say ye of him, whom *the Father* hath sanctified, and *sent into the world*, Thou blasphemest; because I said, *I am the Son of God?*

37. If I do not the works of my Father, believe me not.

38. But if I do, though ye believe not me, *believe the works*: that ye may know, and believe, that *the Father is in me*, and I in him.

39. Therefore they sought again to take him: but *he escaped* out of their hand

In verse 30 of John 10, Jesus definitively states that Jehovah and he *are one.* So, why in sanity did the Christians *concoct their pseudo "Holy Trinity" (father, son, and Holy Ghost), when Jesus states that there is only one, eh?* Jesus never told anyone that *he was Jehovah himself*. He merely stated that *Jehovah was in him* as is the case with *every living creature* upon the face of the entire Earth. Further, verses 34 and 35 of John 10, are the *definition and explanation* of the "Son of God" terminology used by Jesus. His reference to "written in your laws" in verse 34 can be found in the "Psalms" of *David*:

Bible / Psalm 82

1. God standeth in the congregation of the mighty; he judgeth *among the gods*.

6. I have said, *YE ARE GODS*; and *ALL OF YOU ARE CHILDREN OF THE MOST HIGH*.

7. But ye shall *die like men*, and *fall* like one of the princes.

Verse 6 of Psalm 82 definitively and resoundingly delivers the *context* for the "Son of God" terminology used by Jesus. He did not intend for anyone to *misinterpret or misrepresent* his "Son of God" declaration, nor did he intend for anyone to believe that *he was the ONLY "Son of God."* As I've previously relayed, Jesus was *ever cunning in his use of semantics*, indeed.

In the preceding verses, *David* relays that *all human beings (males and females) are the children of Lord Jehovah*. This is consistent with the decrees of the prophets before him. Therefore, any verses that are *in opposition or contradict* the decrees of The Lord in verse 6 of Psalm 82 have been *diabolically inserted* by demons in skin suits; here is an example of my charge:

Bible / John 13

13. Ye call me *Master and Lord*: and ye say well; *for so I am*.

Now, here is the *rectification of the LIE* in verse 13 of John 13:

Bible / John 20

16. Jesus saith unto her, Mary. She turned herself, and saith unto him, _Rabboni_; which is to say, _Master_.

17. Jesus saith unto her, Touch me not; for I am not yet ascended to my Father: but go to my brethren, and say unto them, I ascend unto my Father, _AND YOUR FATHER_; and to MY GOD, _AND YOUR GOD_.

Bible / Matthew 23

8. But be not ye called _Rabbi_: for _one is your Master, even Christ_; and all ye are brethren.

9. And _call no man your father_ upon the earth: for _one is your Father, which is in heaven_.

10. _Neither be ye called masters: for one is your Master_, even Christ.

As is clear, even the _wife of Jesus (Mary Magdalene)_ was of the _stiff-necked rebellious or defiant_. Regardless of the number of times Jesus commanded his disciples to _stop referring to him as Rabboni or Master, they stubbornly continued to do so._ In verses 8 and 10 of Matthew 23, Jesus definitively states that _even Christ has a master_ who is The Lord of the Cosmos. Consequently, his wife and his disciples _concocted and believed their own mythology_ regarding Jesus _against his resounding command not to do so_; their _myths_ regarding Jesus have endured unto this very day.

Bible / Matthew 6

95

6. But thou, when thou prayest, enter into thy closet, and when thou hast shut thy door, *pray to thy Father* which is in secret; and *thy Father* which seeth in secret shall reward thee openly.

7. But when ye pray, use not *vain repetitions*, as the *heathen* do: for they think that they shall be heard for their much speaking.

8. Be not ye therefore like unto them: for *your Father* knoweth what things ye have need of, before ye ask him.

Consequently, Jesus *never elevated himself above the other mere mortal human beings* of the earth, whatsoever. Jesus precisely and definitively tells his wife Mary Magdalene that *Jehovah is her father and her God, same as Jehovah is his father and his God*. Henceforth, alleged Christians have *stubbornly created a fantasy* regarding Jesus, and have *perpetuated their fantasy for some 2,000 years*. These perpetually rebellious alleged Christians have simply forced Jesus to be *greater than he made himself*. Here is The Holy Qur'an on the "Son of God:"

Holy Qur'an / Surah 5

73. Certainly they disbelieve who say: *Allah is the third of the three. And there is no god but One God.* And if they desist not from what they say, a painful chastisement will surely befall such of them as disbelieve.

74. Will they not then turn to Allah and ask His forgiveness? And Allah is Forgiving, Merciful.

Verse 73 of Surah 5 serves to *annihilate* the "Holy Trinity" (Father, Son, and Holy Ghost) of Christianity. Allah (or Jehovah, God, etc.) declares himself to be *the one and only Lord* and Creator of the Universe, which is consistent with *all scriptures before the birth of Jesus*; he was *only a prophet* of Jehovah, nothing more:

Holy Qur'an / Surah 5

17. They indeed *disbelieve* who say: Surely, *Allah — He is the Messiah, son of Mary*. Say: Who then could control anything as against Allah when He wished to *destroy the Messiah, son of Mary, and his mother and all those on the earth?* And Allah's is the kingdom of the heavens and the earth and what is between them. He creates what He pleases. And Allah is Possessor of power over all things.

Bible / John 3

15. That whosoever believeth in him should not perish, but have eternal life.

16. For God so loved the world, that he gave *his only begotten Son*, that whosoever believeth in him should not perish, but have everlasting life.

18. He that believeth on him is not condemned: but he that believeth not is condemned already, because he hath not believed in the name of *the only begotten Son of God himself*.

Merriam Webster's Dictionary / BEGET or BEGOTTEN:

1 : *to procreate* as the father : <u>SIRE</u>

2 : to produce especially as an effect or outgrowth

Holy Qur'an / Surah 112

1. Say: He, Allah, is *One*.

2. Allah is He on Whom all depend.

3. *He begets not, nor is He begotten*;

4. And none is like Him!

Praise The Lord for the whole and complete truth from the preceding verses of The Holy Qur'an regarding this "only begotten son" nonsense that was *inserted into The Bible* by demons in human skin suits. *Lord Jehovah did not beget Jesus, nor did he beget Adam, for neither of them were created by means of Jehovah engaging in physical sexual intercourse with a human woman of the Earth*. Consequently, any verses in The Bible that *contradict* the declarations of the prophets before the birth of Jesus are *satanic lies*, period. Here is further *disgust* from Almighty Jehovah:

Holy Qur'an / Surah 6

101. Wonderful Originator of the heavens and the earth! How could *He have a son when He has no consort?* And He created everything, and He is the Knower of all things.

102. That is Allah, your Lord. There is *no god but He; the Creator of all things*; therefore serve Him, and He has charge of all things.

30. And the Jews say: *Ezra is the son of Allah*; and the Christians say: *The Messiah is the son of Allah*. These are the words of their mouths. They imitate the saying of those who disbelieved before. *Allah's curse be on them!* How they are turned away!

31. They take *their doctors of law and their monks for Lords* besides Allah, and (also) the Messiah, son of Mary. And they were enjoined that they should *serve one God only - there is no god but He*. Be He glorified from what they set up (with Him)!

Holy Qur'an / Surah 19

88. And they say: The Beneficent *has taken to Himself a son*.

89. Certainly you make *an abominable assertion!*

90. The heavens may almost be rent thereat, and the earth cleave asunder, and the mountains fall down in pieces,

91. That *they ascribe a son* to the Beneficent!

92. And it is *not worthy* of the Beneficent that he should *take to Himself a son*.

93. There is none in the heavens and the earth but comes to the Beneficent *as a servant*.

Aye, Christians *make an abominable assertion with their Holy Trinity* rhetoric, indeed. Here is even greater absurdity regarding their *worship of Jesus*, which I promised to revisit:

Bible / John 9

35. Jesus heard that they had cast him out; and when he had found him, he said unto him, Dost thou *believe on the Son of God*?

36. He answered and said, Who is he, *Lord*, that I might believe on him?

37. And Jesus said unto him, Thou hast both *seen him*, and it is *he that talketh with thee*.

38. And he said, *Lord*, I believe. And *he worshipped him*.

Now, the word "Lord" in verse 36 of John 9, is the *siren or red alert* that the *entire passage was inserted by Satan* and his demons for the purpose of *distortion and confusion*. How in sanity could the individual refer to Jesus as "Lord," *yet (simultaneously) not know that he was "The Lord" until Jesus told him so, eh?* Satan and his demon brethren may *fool most of the Earth* with their *inserted contradictory concoctions*, but a handful of us *see your evil deeds*.

Since Jesus has delivered his *actual definition* and rationale for "Son of God," we now know that *he could not have instructed a single soul anywhere in that Bible to WORSHIP HIM*, whatsoever. Therefore, any who elected or chose to worship him were either *rebellious deviants*, or *completely void of sanity*. The same holds true for the alleged Christians of this modern day. Here again is The Bible rectifier:

Holy Qur'an / Surah3

51. Surely *Allah is my Lord and your Lord*, so serve Him. This is the *right path*.

116. And when Allah will say: O Jesus, son of Mary, didst thou say to men, *Take me and my mother for two gods besides Allah?* He will say: Glory be to Thee! it was not for me to say what I had no right to (say). If I had said it, Thou wouldst indeed have known it. Thou knowest what is in my mind, and I know not what is in Thy mind. Surely Thou art the great Knower of the unseen.

117. I said to them naught save as *Thou didst command me: Serve Allah, my Lord and your Lord*; and I was a witness of them so long as I was among them, but when Thou didst cause me to die, Thou wast the Watcher over them. And Thou art Witness of all things.

118. If Thou chastise them, surely they are Thy servants; and if Thou protect them, surely Thou art the Mighty, the Wise.

Again, Jesus commanded *the eternally rebellious NOT to worship him*, but their true father Jehovah. However, even his disciples were of the *vehemently defiant in their worship of him*.

Bible / Luke 13

25. When once the master of the house is risen up, and hath shut to the door, and ye begin to stand without, and to knock at the

door, saying, *Lord, Lord, open unto us;* and he shall answer and say unto you, *I know you not whence ye are:*

26. Then shall ye begin to say, *We have eaten and drunk in thy presence, and thou hast taught in our streets.*

27. But he shall say, I tell you, I know you not whence ye are; *depart from me, all ye workers of iniquity.*

28. There shall be weeping and gnashing of teeth, when *ye shall see Abraham, and Isaac, and Jacob, and all the prophets,* in the kingdom of God, and *you yourselves thrust out!*

Holy Qur'an / Surah 4

159. And there is none of the People of the Book but will believe in this before his death; and on the day of Resurrection *he will be a witness against them.*

PAUL & BARNABUS INVENT CHRISTIANITY

Consequently, Jesus himself will *be a witness* against all alleged Christians when they stand before Jehovah for judgment in the realm unseen by mortals. Actually, *Jesus did not tell any human beings to refer to themselves as Christians in the first place.* This term was *concocted and inserted* into The Bible by *two demons* in human skin suits:

Bible / Acts 11

25. Then departed *Barnabas* to Tarsus, for to seek *Saul (Paul):*
26. And when he had found him, he brought him unto Antioch. And it came to pass, that a whole year they assembled themselves with the church, and taught much people. And the <u>disciples were called Christians first in Antioch</u>.

We (yet again) have the *stiff-necked rebellious (Barnabas and Saul = Paul) INVENTING that which Jesus did not relay to anyone, anywhere, anytime. Jesus was not a Christian* and neither should his true followers refer to themselves as such. However, he will be a "witness against them" in the realm unseen, indeed.

To further establish his opposition toward any who desired to *worship him*, he offers this magnificent endearment to Lord Jehovah:

JESUS PRAYS TO JEHOVAH

Bible / Matthew 6

9. After this manner therefore pray ye: *Our Father which art in heaven*, Hallowed be thy name.

10. Thy kingdom come, Thy will be done in earth, as it is in heaven.

11. Give us this day our daily bread.

12. And forgive us our debts, as we forgive our debtors.

13. And lead us not into temptation, but deliver us from evil: For thine is the kingdom, and the power, and the glory, for ever. Amen.

A similar endearment to Jehovah is offered by the arc-angel *Gabriel* in The Holy Qur'an. This passage is known as "Al-Fatihah" or "The Opening:"

Holy Qur'an / Surah 1

1. Praise be to Allah, The Lord of the worlds,

2. The Beneficent, the Merciful,

3. Master of the day of Requital.

4. Thee do we serve and Thee do we beseech for help.

5. Guide us on the right path,

6. The path of those upon whom Thou hast bestowed favours,

7. Not those upon whom wrath is brought down, nor those who go astray.

Beautiful, indeed. Here is yet another consistent declaration of Jesus regarding the one to be worshiped which is *contrary to the rebellious Christian fantasy*:

Bible / John 4

19. The woman saith unto him, Sir, I perceive that *thou art a prophet*.

20. Our fathers worshipped in this mountain; and ye say, that in Jerusalem is the place where men ought to worship.

21. Jesus saith unto her, Woman, believe me, the hour cometh, when ye shall neither in this mountain, nor yet at Jerusalem, *worship the Father*.

22. *Ye worship ye know not what*: we know what we worship: for salvation is of the Jews.

23. But the hour cometh, and now is, when the true worshippers shall *worship the Father in spirit and in truth*: for *the Father* seeketh such *to worship him*.

As is clear in the preceding verses, *Jesus did not tell a single soul to worship him*, period. Jesus was dead right in his prophesy of future generations *not worshipping Jehovah on a mountain, nor in Jerusalem.* His "ye worship ye know not what" terminology is applicable to the Christians of this modern day. They worship the *mere image of a man (Jesus) that has been diabolically manufactured* by demons in skin suits, for there are *no photographs or busts of stone* in the image of the Jesus of some 2,000 years ago in existence today. Therefore, Christians *do not know what they worship* as Jesus prophesied. Any Christians who pray to anyone or anything besides *Lord Jehovah (alone)* are *defiant deviants,* indeed. Let us now focus upon the *alleged death and resurrection of Jesus:*

THE PRESUMED DEATH OF JESUS

Bible / Matthew 26

36. Then cometh Jesus with them unto a place called Gethsemane, and saith unto the disciples, Sit ye here, *while I go and pray yonder*.

37. And he took with him Peter and the two sons of Zebedee, and began to be *sorrowful and very heavy*.

38. Then saith he unto them, My soul is *exceeding sorrowful, even unto death*: tarry ye here, and watch with me.

39. And he went a little farther, and *fell on his face, and prayed*, saying, O my Father, if it be possible, *let this cup pass from me*: nevertheless not *as I will*, but *as thou wilt*.

40. And he cometh unto the disciples, and findeth them asleep, and saith unto Peter, What, could ye not watch with me one hour?

41. Watch and pray, that ye enter not into temptation: the spirit indeed is willing, but the flesh is weak.

42. He went away again the *second time, and prayed*, saying, O my Father, if this cup may *not pass away from me*, except I drink it, *thy will be done.*

43. And he came and found them asleep again: for their eyes were heavy.

44. And he left them, and *went away again, and prayed the third time*, saying the same words.

Let us venture into the realm of *common sense* once again. If you are Christian, do you actually believe that Lord Jehovah would allow *Jesus (whom he loved so dearly) to be murdered* by his earthly enemies? No, indeed. Did Lord Jehovah allow his other major prophets (*Noah, Abraham, David, Moses, Muhammad, and so on*) to be *murdered* by his earthly enemies? No, indeed. In the preceding verses, we have Jesus in such *extreme agony* regarding his impending crucifixion that he removes himself from the presence of his disciples to *pray not once, but three times in the same evening.* Consequently, if you are Christian and believe that Lord Jehovah *mercilessly* allowed Jesus to be killed on the cross, you are gravely mistaken. Let us define the term *crucify*:

Merriam Webster's Dictionary / CRUCIFY:

1 : *to put to death* by nailing or binding the wrists or hands and feet to a cross.

Consequently, Jesus was *bound and nailed* to the cross, but technically *not "crucified"* because *he did not die* on the cross. Here is the reasoning for my declaration:

Bible / Matthew 27

34. They gave him *vinegar to drink mingled with gall*: and when he had tasted thereof, he would not drink.

45. Now from the sixth hour there was darkness over all the land unto the ninth hour.

46. And about the ninth hour Jesus *cried with a loud voice, saying, Eli, Eli, lama sabachthani? that is to say, My God, my God, why hast thou forsaken me?*

47. Some of them that stood there, when they heard that, said, This man calleth for Elias.

48. And straightway one of them ran, and took a spunge, and *filled it with vinegar*, and put it on a reed, and gave him to drink.

49. The rest said, Let be, let us see whether Elias will come to save him.

50. Jesus, when he had *cried again with a loud voice, yielded up the ghost.*

51. And, behold, the veil of the temple was rent in twain from the top to the bottom; and the earth did quake, and the rocks rent;

52. And the graves were opened; and many bodies of the saints which slept arose

In verse 46 of Matthew 27, Jesus had a *lapse of faith and harbored rage* against Lord Jehovah for allowing him to be *so brutally tortured and ridiculed* by his enemies. After praying so intensely, how then could The Lord abandon or forsake him? The answer that Jesus sought lies in the <u>Book of Job</u> *in The Bible*. The prophet *Job* also suffered tremendous afflictions that were sanctioned by The Lord of the Worlds. Consequently, just as Job's faith was *diminished to the point that he cursed Lord Jehovah*, so it was with Jesus on the cross. Here is The Holy Qur'an regarding *affliction or suffering*:

Holy Qur'an / Surah 29

1. I, Allah, am the best Knower.

2. Do men think that they will *be left alone* on saying, We *believe*, and *will not be tried?*

3. And indeed *We tried those before them*, so Allah will certainly know *those who are true* and He will know the liars.

In light of this, all believers will *endure trials and tribulation*; some to a worse degree than others. Jesus was ignorant as to the *master plan* within The Real Mind of God:

Holy Qur'an / Surah 8

30. And when those who disbelieved *devised plans* against thee that they might confine thee or slay thee or drive thee away –

111

and *they devised plans* and *Allah, too, had arranged a plan;* and *Allah is the best of planners!*

Consequently, Jesus was merely *unaware* that Lord Jehovah *had no intention of allowing him to die on that cross.* Jesus was merely rendered *comatose or seemingly dead* after his crucifixion:

Holy Qur'an / Surah 4

157. And for their saying: *We have killed the Messiah, Jesus, son of Mary,* the messenger of Allah, and *they killed him not, nor did they cause his death on the cross, but he was made to appear to them as such.* And certainly those who differ therein are in doubt about it. They have *no knowledge about it, but only follow a conjecture,* and they *killed him not for certain:*

158. Nay, Allah exalted him in His presence. And Allah is ever Mighty, Wise.

Yeah, *no one knew that Jesus was alive after his crucifixion* save for The Lord himself. However, *Pontius Pilate had his doubts* regarding the death of Jesus, for it normally took *days* for a man to physically die on a cross. Yet, Jesus was *perceived* as dead in a matter of *mere hours:*

Bible / Mark 15

43. Joseph of Arimathaea, an honourable counsellor, which also waited for the kingdom of God, came, and went in boldly unto Pilate, and craved the body of Jesus.

44. And *Pilate marvelled if he were already dead:* and calling unto him the centurion, he asked him whether he had been any while dead.

45. And when he knew it of the centurion, he *gave the body to Joseph.*

Again, Jesus was only *perceived as dead.* The following may be the cause of the *comatose state* of Jesus that *fooled all living* in that day:

Bible / Deuteronomy 32

32. For their vine is of the vine of Sodom, and of the fields of Gomorrah: their grapes are *grapes of gall,* their clusters are *bitter:*

33. Their *wine is the poison* of dragons, and the cruel *venom of asps.*

Bible / Job 20

14. Yet his meat in his bowels is turned, it is the *gall of asps within him.*

In verse 34 of Matthew 27, the *vinegar mixed with gall is a form of poison* that is associated with the *venom of asp snakes.* This poison that Jesus drank induced a *comatose physical state.* A coma would be the explanation for the following:

Bible / John 19

31. The Jews therefore, because it was the preparation, that *the bodies should not remain upon the cross on the sabbath day,* (for

that sabbath day was an high day,) besought Pilate that *their legs might be broken*, and that they might be taken away.

32. Then came the soldiers, and brake the legs of the first, and of the other which was crucified with him.

33. But when they came to Jesus, and *saw that he was dead already, they brake not his legs*:

34. But one of the soldiers *with a spear pierced his side*, and forthwith came there out *blood and water*.

35. And he that saw it bare record, and his record is true: and he knoweth that he saith true, that ye might believe.

36. For these things were done, that the scripture should be fulfilled, *A bone of him shall not be broken*.

37. And again another scripture saith, They shall look on him *whom they pierced*.

Aye, Jesus suffered *no broken bones*. Therefore, it would have been easy for him to *physically walk* out of his tomb. Further, when the solider pierced the side of Jesus with that spear, Jesus *did not flinch* in the least. This bolsters my premise of a *comatose state*. However, if you believe that my hypothesis is farfetched or *impossible*, here is the *scientific data* for my claim:

Columbia Encyclopedia / <u>CATALEPSY</u>:

Pathological condition characterized by a *loss of consciousness* accompanied by *<u>rigidity of muscles that keeps limbs in any</u>*

position in which they are placed. Attacks vary from *several minutes to days* and occur in a variety of *clinical syndromes*, most frequently in schizophrenia, *epilepsy*, and hysteria.

Encyclopedia of Occultism and Parapsychology: A condition involving the sudden suspension of sensation and volition and the partial *suspension of vital functions*. The body assumes *a rigid appearance, sometimes mistaken for death*, and the victim *remains unconscious* throughout the attack. On occasion, the cataleptic state may be marked by symptoms of intense mental excitement and by apparently volitional speech and action. Sometimes the symptoms are hardly distinguishable from those of hysteria. The period covered by the attack may vary *from a few minutes to several days*, although the latter occurs only in exceptional cases. An attack may recur, however, on only trifling provocation in the absence of strong resistance by the victim. Catalepsy is associated with schizophrenia and hysteria, and there is reason to believe that it *can be self-induced* in certain cases. Eastern fakirs have been known to cast themselves into a *cataleptic sleep lasting for months*, and cases have even been reported where they permitted themselves to be *buried, being exhumed* when the grass had grown over their graves. Some forms of *trance induced by hypnotism* appear similar to the *cataleptic state*.

In light of the preceding regarding *CATALEPSY*, *no human being possessed the knowledge of the physical death of Jesus on the cross with certainty in that day*, *and there is no human being in this day that can verify that Jesus physically died on the cross*. A "*cataleptic sleep*" was what Jesus was referring to when he said this regarding *Lazurus* and the *alleged dead maid*:

Bible / John 11

4. When Jesus heard that, he said, *This sickness is not unto death*, but for the glory of God, that the Son of God might be glorified thereby.

11. These things said he: and after that he saith unto them, Our friend Lazarus *sleepeth*; but I go, that I may *awake him out of sleep*.

12. Then said his disciples, Lord, if he sleep, he shall do well.

13. Howbeit Jesus spake of his death: but they thought that he had spoken of *taking of rest in sleep*.

14. Then said Jesus unto them plainly, Lazarus is dead.

Bible / Matthew 9

24. He said unto them, Give place: for *the maid is not dead, but sleepeth*. And they laughed him to scorn.

Cataleptic Sleep is the *logical conclusion*, indeed. Here are the prophesies (verses) regarding Jesus that are referenced in verses 36 and 37 of John 19:

20. He keepeth *all his bones: not one of them is broken.*

10. And I will pour upon the house of David, and upon the inhabitants of Jerusalem, the spirit of grace and of supplications: and *they shall look upon me whom they have pierced*, and they shall mourn for him, as one mourneth for his only son, and shall be in bitterness for him, as one that is in bitterness for his firstborn.

Here are other prophecies that have been fulfilled regarding the crucifixion of Jesus:

16. For dogs have compassed me: the *assembly of the wicked* have inclosed me: *they pierced my hands and my feet.*

17. I may tell all my bones: they *look* and *stare upon me.*

18. They *part my garments among them, and cast lots* upon my vesture.

35. And *they crucified him, and parted his garments, casting lots*: that it might be fulfilled which was spoken by the prophet, They parted my garments among them, and upon my vesture did they cast lots.

36. And sitting down *they watched him there.*

Let us now add the final piece to the puzzle that occurred *before the alleged resurrection* of Jesus:

38. And after this *Joseph of Arimathaea, being a disciple of Jesus, but secretly* for fear of the Jews, besought Pilate that he might *take away the body of Jesus*: and Pilate gave him leave. He came therefore, and *took the body* of Jesus.

Aye, the plot thickens! We now have a Jesus *with no broken bones, a puncture wound in his side, a poisonous drink of gall, and a body that is whisked away by an honorable disciple of his (Joseph of Arimathaea) before anyone has an opportunity to fully examine it. Consequently, no one was certain that Jesus physically died on the cross as The Holy Qur'an declares*. Hence, all in this day merely *speculate about his death on the cross*, nothing more.

SECRET DISCIPLES OF JESUS

Since I had promised to return to *Mary Magdalene* and *other disciples* of Jesus (besides "The Twelve") in verse 38 of John 19, notice that *Joseph of Arimathaea is a secret or unknown disciple of Jesus*. This is highly significant, for most Christians *only acknowledge and promote "The Twelve"* disciples of Jesus to the masses; they *completely dismiss* even the possibility of *the wife of Jesus (Mary Magdalene) being a disciple of his*. However, while "The Twelve" were busy *cowering in dark corners for fear of suffering the identical fate of Jesus (torture and crucifixion)*, the "disciple whom Jesus loved" (*his stepbrother James*) and *the disciple who was his wife (Mary Magdalene) were standing fearlessly by his side even at the very site of his crucifixion*. It is no wonder that Jesus *loved these two devout and courageous disciples*. Actually, Jesus had *many other disciples* besides "The Twelve:"

Bible / Luke 10

1. After these things The Lord *appointed other seventy also*, and sent them two and two before his face into every city and place, whither he himself would come.

17. And *the seventy returned again* with joy, saying, Lord, even the devils are subject unto us through thy name.

As is clear in verses 1 and 17 of Luke 10, Jesus *commanded numerous disciples besides "The Twelve."* Consequently, no human being on earth in this day can definitively declare that *Mary Magdalene was not one of these "Seventy" disciples of Jesus*. Let us now focus upon the *famed resurrection of Jesus*:

THE RESURRECTION OF JESUS

Bible / Mark 16

3. And they said among themselves, Who shall roll us away the stone from the door of the sepulchre?

4. And when they looked, they saw that *the stone was rolled away*: for it was very great.

Here is *uncommon sense*: alleged Christians believe that Jesus *became a spirit or ghost* upon his resurrection. However, if Jesus became an *actual ghost, why in sanity would the giant stone be "rolled away"* as verse 4 of Mark 16 declares? If he were a ghost, he could simply *walk or fly through the stone*, correct? Consequently, the stone being *rolled away* so that Jesus could *exit the tomb does not make an atom of sense*, and a few Christians know this.

Bible / Mark 16

9. Now when Jesus was risen early the first day of the week, *he appeared first to Mary Magdalene*, out of whom he had cast seven devils.

A male's mother is the *primary female* in his life from birth to late teens. She cooks his dinner, washes his clothes, straightens his room, and so on. However, when that male attains adulthood and marries, *his wife becomes the central or primary female in his existence.* Consequently, it is *logical* for Jesus to have appeared *to his wife Mary Magdalene before any other beings* including his mother, Mary.

Bible / Luke 24

5. And as they were afraid, and bowed down their faces to the earth, they said unto them, *Why seek ye the living among the dead?*

Mary Magdalene sought "the living among the dead" because she believed that *Jesus had physically died*, as did all who saw him crucified. However, Jesus *did not physically die* on the cross, as the preceding question in the verse clearly underscores.

Bible / John 20

11. But Mary stood without at the sepulchre weeping: and as she wept, she stooped down, and looked into the sepulchre,

12. And seeth *two angels in white sitting*, the one at the head, and the other at the feet, where *the body of Jesus had lain*.

13. And they say unto her, Woman, why weepest thou? She saith unto them, Because they have taken away my LORD, and I know not where they have laid him.

Here is *uncommon sense (logic or reason)* once again. If Jesus had actually physically died, and had risen after three days as a "holy ghost" (as Christians *ignorantly* proclaim), why in sanity would *he need his three-days dead, petrified (rigor mortis), rotting, physical corpse to leave the tomb*, eh? This does not make *an atom of sense*. What does make sense is that Jesus was *physically alive* when he was placed in the tomb, and he simply *awakened* from his "*cataleptic sleep*" as previously relayed.

Bible / John 20

14. And when she had thus said, she turned herself back, and *saw Jesus standing, and knew not that it was Jesus*.

15. Jesus saith unto her, Woman, why weepest thou? whom seekest thou? *She, supposing him to be the gardener*, saith unto him, Sir, if thou have borne him hence, *tell me where thou hast laid him*, and I will take him away.

We now have Jesus *standing in front of, and speaking directly to his wife*, Mary. However, she cannot see his face, and *mistakes him for a gardener*. If you are familiar with gardening apparel, you have seen gardeners wearing large hats, often with *veils* attached. These veils protect the gardeners' face from wasps, bees, and the like. Consequently, Mary simply *could not see the face of Jesus behind the veil*. This is of tremendous significance, for *why in sanity would Jesus need to disguise himself as a gardener if he were a ghost or no longer of the physical world, eh? Ghosts do not need clothes of the physical world.* Hence, Jesus simply did not want the Jews and Romans *to discover that he had survived his crucifixion.* Therefore, his *gardener costume* was an *excellent disguise* that allowed him to *move among the Jews and Romans undetected.* Jesus was ever the crafty or cunning one, indeed.

Bible / John 20

16. Jesus saith unto her, Mary. She turned herself, and saith unto him, Rabboni; which is to say, Master.

17. Jesus saith unto her, Touch me not; for *I am not yet ascended to my Father*: but go to my brethren, and say unto them, I ascend unto *my Father, and your Father; and to my God, and your God.*

18. Mary Magdalene came and told the disciples that she had seen The Lord, and that he had spoken these things unto her.

Verse 17 of John 20 is *clear and definitive* to those of sanity. Jesus tells his wife that *he is not dead or a ghost*, and that she *should not touch his living, physical body*. There is no further clarification needed, whatsoever.

Bible / Luke 24

15. And it came to pass, that, while they communed together and reasoned, *Jesus himself drew near, and went with them.*

16. But their eyes were holden that they *should not know him.*

17. And he said unto them, What manner of communications are these that ye have one to another, as ye walk, and are sad?

18. And the one of them, whose name was Cleopas, answering said unto him, *Art thou only a stranger in Jerusalem*, and hast not known the things which are come to pass there in these days?

19. And *he said unto them, What things?* And they said unto him, Concerning Jesus of Nazareth, which was *a prophet* mighty in deed and word before God and all the people:

20. And how the chief priests and our rulers delivered him to be condemned to death, and have crucified him.

As relayed earlier in this chapter, Jesus enjoyed *taunting and testing* those in his presence, friend or foe. We know this from: his writing on the ground while his enemies sought to condemn him regarding the adulteress, his verbal joust with Pontius Pilate, his constant parable responses to his disciples, and so on. Therefore, Jesus is merely *having fun or joking* with those who are walking with him in the preceding verses of Luke 24. He is obviously *still in some form of disguise.*

Bible / Luke 24

34. Saying, The Lord is risen indeed, and hath appeared to Simon.

35. And they told what things were done in the way, and how he was known of them in breaking of bread.

36. And as they thus spake, *Jesus himself stood in the midst of them, and saith unto them, Peace be unto you.*

37. But they were terrified and affrighted, and *supposed* that they had *seen a spirit.*

38. And he said unto them, Why are ye troubled? and why do thoughts arise in your hearts?

39. Behold my hands and my feet, that <u>*it is I myself: handle me, and see; for a spirit hath not flesh and bones, as ye see me have*</u>.

40. And when he had thus spoken, *he shewed them his hands and his feet.*

41. And while <u>*they yet believed not for joy, and wondered*</u>, he said unto them, *Have ye here any meat?*

42. And they gave him a piece of a broiled fish, and of an honeycomb.

43. And he took it, and <u>*did eat before them*</u>.

Yeah, the preceding verses are resounding and definitive, indeed. Jesus commanded his *consistently rebellious disciples to touch his "flesh and bones"* so that they would know with certainty that *he did not physically die on the cross.* However, his *perpetually rebellious* disciples "believed not for joy" and *disregarded his decree* as they had done so often in the past. His "a spirit hath not flesh and bones, as ye see me have" declaration in verse 39 of Luke 24, *completely annihilates the* blasphemous *"holy trinity"* rhetoric *of the Christians*. Hence, Jesus himself declared that *he was not a spirit or ghost after his crucifixion*, so he was *not physically dead*. Consequently, any who *despicably persist* in perpetuating the falsehood that *Jesus rose from physical death as a "holy ghost"* (the "holy trinity" fantasy) are as far away from Lord Jehovah, The Real Jesus, and complete truth in The Bible as Pluto is from the Sun.

The "have ye here any meat?" in verse 41 and "he took it and did eat before them" in 43 of Luke 24, further *annihilates the Christian ghost fairy tale* regarding Jesus. Why in sanity *would a ghost crave or hunger for physical food of the physical world,* eh? Have you ever seen a ghost chomping on *a fried chicken leg, or fish and chips?* I think not. So, in conclusion,

JESUS DID NOT COME TO SAVE THE WORLD &

HE DID NOT DIE ON THE CROSS.

GLORY TO LORD JEHOVAH!

BIBLIOGRAPHY

Ali, Maulana (Maulvi) Muhammad (Translator), *The Holy Qur'an*, Woking, Surrey, Islamic Review Office, 1917. (November 16, 2016)

Ben-Yehuda's Pocket Dictionary, Pocket Books 1961, 1964.

Bergen, Peter, *Holy War Inc.*, Free Press, 2001

Bodden, Valerie, *The Bombing of Hiroshima & Nagasaki,* The Creative Company, 2007

Bregman, Ahron, *Israel's Wars: A History Since 1947*, London: Routledge, 2002.

"Catalepsy." *Encyclopedia of Occultism and Parapsychology*. The Gale Group, Inc, 2001. *Answers.com* 06 Jul. 2007.

"Catalepsy." *The Columbia Encyclopedia,* 6th ed. New York: Columbia University Press, 2001-04.

James, M.R. (Translation and Notes), *The Apocryphal New Testament*, Oxford: Clarendon Press, 1924

King James, *The Apocrypha*, Press Syndicate of the University of Cambridge, (August 11, 1983)

King James, *The Bible (1611)*, Hendrickson Publishers, (June 1, 2003)

Kirby, Peter (Translator). *Infancy Gospel of Thomas*, Early Christian Writings, 2011

"*Merriam-Webster Online Dictionary*" copyright © 2005 by Merriam-Webster, Incorporated

Nelson, Thomas (Translator), *The Lost Books of the Bible; and the Forgotten Books of* Eden, LB Press, (January 1, 1963)

ABOUT THIS AUTHOR

Prof. Robert Stewart

is a retired clandestine operative who was recruited, while a student at U.C. Berkeley, into a special program for humans with Paranormal gifts. His fields of expertise are child extraction from cults, world religions, science, and the Occult. Musician was his deep cover or camouflage life.

Stewart is also multi-instrumentalist (saxophones, piano, flute, drum, vocals, etc.), composer, producer, educator, soldier, Martial Artist, Scientist-Metaphysicist, theologian and author. His two major label albums ("The Force" and "In the Gutta") were for Quincy Jones and Qwest/Warner Bros. records. He is known for his unique – personal sound and remarkably inventive improvisations declares Los Angeles Times journalist Bill Kohlhaase, as the lead tenor saxophonist on the Pulitzer Prize winning "Blood on the Fields" by trumpeter Wynton Marsalis, and as the protegé of saxophonist Pharoah Sanders. Jazz critic Jason Ankeny declared Stewart to be one of the most impressive jazz saxophonists to emerge at the end of the 20th century. Drummer Billy Higgins refers to Stewart as "perhaps the most important young artist to come along in decades."

EARLY LIFE

Robert Darrin Stewart was born on August 17, 1969 in Oakland, California. His biological father (Robert Stewart III) is a San Francisco Conservatory trained flutist and trumpeter who performed with the legendary R&B group "The Whispers" during the late 1960's, and musical director for the 1950's Pop vocalist Bobby Freeman during the 1970's. Stewart's mother (Jackie Mae Syas) was a computer analysts born in Lake Charles, Louisiana. His step-father (Clifton Cecil Patrick) was a truck driver and agriculturalist born in Lynchburg, Virginia.

Stewart's mother began teaching him to read from the Holy Qur'an of Islam from the time that he was 3 years old; The Bible (Judaism and Christianity) was his next reading task. After these, Stewart began his personal studies of the other 4 major religions of the world: Buddhism, Hinduism, Taoism, and Confucianism. Consequently, Theology was his early foundation.

In the early 1980's, Oakland underwent a metamorphosis; from being the city that produced such influential musical dynasties as Sly and The Family Stone and The Tower of Power, and such radical social revolutionaries as Huey P. Newton (founder) and The Black Panther Party, to a city that is one of North America's most notorious gang war zones; riddled with crack cocaine, military assault weapons, and mass murder. In the 21st century, Oakland remains one of the top 5 most dangerous - notorious cites in the United States. Consequently, it is a genuine miracle that Stewart was able to rise from the flames of this netherworld as a Phoenix in the jazz idiom.

Were it not for Stewart's uncle (David Williams) giving him a flute that he'd acquired, Stewart may not have ever played any kind of musical instrument. Stewart's mother bought a flute method book for Stewart's new toy. He then began to teach himself to read music from this book at 11 years of age. He was the first chair flute soloist for all of his high school and junior high school band years. Playing the flute was merely a hobby for him, for his primary passion was Basketball during all of his grade school years. He's 6'4" tall, and played the shooting guard position for the Fremont High School Varsity team (coached by Michael Marcoulis and Sheridan James) during his junior and senior years. He simply played music to get the credit to graduate; no interest beyond this. In fact, he was most interested in Rap music. When not on the basketball court, he rapped under the alias "Mix Master D" and spent his time practicing mixing and scratching albums on stereo turntables. Of course, these activities attracted seedy company in his "hood" (neighborhood). He admits to having to hide his flute in his gym bag each school day, so that his murderous gangster friends wouldn't know that he played an instrument. His high school music teacher (Donald Ramsey) saw the tremendous potential of Stewart, and would harass him daily about playing jazz. However, Stewart refused to listen to his teacher, and would cut his class regularly in order to play basketball.

The summer after his graduation from Fremont High School, he was surfing his radio for his favorite Rap music station, and stumbled upon an individual playing the tenor saxophone at such a rapid pace it stunned the teenager. This saxophonist was John Coltrane playing the song "Russian Lullaby." The next song on the station was "All Too Soon" played by tenor saxophonist Ben Webster. The contrast in sound between these two men playing the same instrument fascinated Stewart. He then remembered his high school teacher's words and (from that moment in time) his jazz destiny was set into motion.

After the summer of 1986, Stewart began to frequent jam sessions in the classroom of Oakland - Bay Area piano legend Ed Kelly at Laney College. It was there that he met two Jazz saxophone titans; Pharoah Sanders and Joshua Redman. He developed a friendship with both of these giants. Pharoah passed Stewart a note during one class session that read: "come to my house tomorrow. I'll help you with your horn." Stewart accepted the offer and the two remain brothers to this day. Stewart also frequented neighborhood jam sessions in Oakland, California. He met and performed with many Jazz greats at these sessions including: Johnny Coles (trumpet), Frank Fischer (trumpet), Mondre Moffett (trumpet), Junius Courtney (trumpet), Ambrose Akinmusire (trumpet), Tricky Lofton (trombone), John Handy (sax), Pony Poindexter (sax), Frank Morgan (sax), Morris Atchinson (sax), Bobby Forte (sax), Jules Broussard (sax), Merl Sanders (piano), Buddy Montgomery (piano), Vijay Iyer (piano), Phil Reeder (piano), Jackie Ivory (organ), Eddie Moore (drums), Donald Bailey (drums), David Garabaldi (drums), Mike Clark (drums), Smiley Winters (drums), Jimmy Robinson (drums), Wyatt Ruther (bass), Herbie Lewis (bass) Frank Biner (guitar) Ledisi (vocalist), Ernie Andrews (vocalist) and many others.

PERFORMANCE CAREER

In 1987, Stewart began leading his own band (The Robert Stewart Experience) at such world-renowned venues as Yoshi's and the San Francisco Jazz Festival due to the efforts made by his manager at the time, filmmaker D. Channsin Berry. He also became one of the most sought-after sidemen in the Bay Area. His first major sideman gig was with avant-garde sax giant Chico Freeman, pianist George Cables, and drummer Eddie Moore in 1988. His next sideman gig that year was with piano legend Freddie Redd of Jackie McLean's band. Trumpet colossus Wynton Marsalis first met and performed with Stewart on this gig.

In 1989, he received a call from trumpet icon Donald Byrd to perform with his group. That same year, he made his first sojourn to New York to perform with Winard and Philip Harper of "The Harper Brothers." While there, he also performed with trumpet legend Eddie Henderson. In 1990, he went back to New York and performed with the iconic composer/arranger/saxophonist Benny Golson and trombonist Tom McIntosh. He also played with trumpet dynamo Roy Hargrove for the first of many times unto this day. Upon his return home to San Francisco, he began working with vocal sensation Mary Stallings and pianist Merrill Hoover. He also worked regularly with "The Grateful Dead" long time pianist Merl Saunders and bassist Wyatt Ruther of Errol Garner's band.

In 1991, Stewart received a phone call from drum legend Max Roach to perform (a saxophone & drums duo) at U.C. Berkeley. He performed with Max Roach's full ensemble a few months later. Stewart also performed at an award ceremony for Be-Bop founding father Dizzy Gillespie. Mr. Gillespie asked Stewart to perform with his band several months later. In 1992, Stewart performed with Jazz legends: McCoy Tyner (piano), Bobby Hutcherson (vibes), Freddie Hubbard (trumpet), Milt Jackson (vibes), Billy Higgins (drums), and organ phenomenon Jimmy Smith. Stewart also joined the Los Angeles based group "Black Note" for an eight-month stint, and performed with trombonist Delfeayo Marsalis and drummer Brian Blade that same year.

In 1993, Stewart was asked to tour with the New York based group "The Harper Brothers" led by drummer Winard Harper. This would be his first National band tour. Following this tour, he remained in New York and performed with vocal legend Etta Jones, saxophonist Donald Harrison, pianist Cyrus Chestnut, saxophonist Billy Mitchell, trumpeter Doc Cheatham, saxophonist George Kelly, and pianist Chris Anderson.

In 1994, Stewart's regular group in San Francisco included Bay Area piano and organ legend Ed Kelly. They would be joined by such legends as: saxophonists George Coleman, Pharoah Sanders, Teddy Edwards, David Murray, John Handy, Big Jay McNeely, Hadley Caliman, and vocalist Ernie Andrews. Stewart also performed with Blues legend John Lee Hooker often at Jack's (on Fillmore St.) in San Francisco. However, Stewart's highest profile engagement of 1994 came after receiving a phone call from trumpet titan Wynton Marsalis to join his newly formed "Wynton Marsalis Big Band" (known today as the "Lincoln Center Jazz Orchestra") to perform the world-premiere of his now historic oratorio "Blood On The Fields" at The Lincoln Center in New York. The other members of this 13-piece all-star band included jazz legends: Jon Hendricks (vocal), Cassandra Wilson (vocal), Jon Faddis (trumpet), James Carter (sax), Marcus Printup (trumpet), Eric Reed (piano), Herlin Riley (drums), Wycliff Gordon (trombone), Regina Carter (violin) and several others. The two-night engagement was hosted by Ed Bradley of "60 minutes." The engagements received rave reviews, and eventually won Wynton the esteemed Pulitzer Prize; the only piece in jazz history to receive an honor of this magnitude by a living composer. Stewart remained a member of the Lincoln Center Jazz Orchestra from 1994 to 1998. This band would be his first international touring experience.

By the end of 1994, Stewart began touring nationally under his own name. He also met and performed with his second great mentor (after Phaorah Sanders); sax juggernaut Eddie Harris. Stewart was like a son to Harris, so he would constantly relay information to Stewart. The two were inseparable until Eddie's untimely death in 1996.

From 1995 to 1997, Stewart performed with saxophonist Branford Marsalis, pianists Kenny Kirkland and Marcus Roberts, drum titan Jeff "Tain" Watts, bassist Ray Drummond, Kirk Hammett (lead guitarist for the iconic rock group "Metallica"), Billie Joe Armstrong (founder of legendary rock band "Green Day"), drummer Zigaboo Modeliste (founding member of the Funk band "The Meters"), and with vocal legends Jon Hendricks and Les McCann inside Alcatraz Island Penitentiary.

From 1998 to 1999, Stewart performed with piano greats Barry Harris and Horrace Tapscott, Avant-garde saxophonist Sonny Simmons, and drum legend Billy Higgins in a series of live concerts for the Museum of Contemporary Art in Los Angeles. His most prestigious performance was for President Bill Clinton and First Lady Hillary Clinton at a Democratic Fund Raiser in Woodside, California in 1998.

From 2000 to the present, Stewart has performed with luminaries of many music genres including: saxophonists Arthur Blythe, Chico Freeman, and Bobby Watson, drummers Marcus Bailor (Yellowjackets), Victor Lewis, Terri Lynn Carrington (Arsenio Hall), keyboardists Greg Philingains (Michael Jackson), Felton Pilate (Confunkshun), vocalist Lenny Williams (Tower of Power), and organists Rhoda Scott, Trudy Pitts, and Chester Thompson (Tower of Power).

RECORDING CAREER

In 1994, Stewart recorded the first album of his career ("Judgement") in Los Angeles for World Stage Records at the behest of drum icon Billy Higgins who owned the label. The recording featured Billy Higgins, pianist Eric Reed, and bassist Mark Shelby. The debut recording for the 24-year-old received rave reviews from the jazz world. Jazz writer Scott Yanow of All Music Guide and L.A. Jazz Scene wrote: "Tenor saxophonist Robert Stewart's debut release is quite unusual. Rarely have I heard a young player sound so laid back and relaxed. Even on the up-tempo tunes, Stewart is often content to emphasize his warm tone and to hold long notes, taking his time to get his message across. Fortunately, he does have something of his own to say, so listeners more used to young turks forcing out as many notes as possible will at first go through a bit of culture shock before warming up to this admirable effort."

In that same year, Stewart met his manager Dennis Sullivan who also managed the Los Angeles Jazz group Black-Note. Dennis asked recording industry titan Sergio Veschi (founder and owner of the prestigious Red Records label of Italy) to sign Stewart. They reached an agreement to do one recording entitled "Beautiful Love Ballads" (originally titled "Beautiful Love"). Although it was recorded in 1994, it wasn't released until 1998. This recording was also well received by jazz critics; one even described Stewart as the most lyrical and melodic saxophone improviser of his generation.

In 1995, Stewart met Jazz enthusiast Craig Morton who became his new manager. Morton convinced music industry icon Quincy Jones (and his record label president Jim Swindel) to sign Stewart to his Qwest/Warner Bros. record label. Stewart's first outing for Mr. Jones was entitled "In The Gutta." Saxophone legend Dave Liebman took a blindfold test for JazzTimes magazine.

Stewart's recording was played, and Liebman swore that Stewart was the legendary R&B tenor-man Red Prysock or Sam "The Man" Taylor. When Liebman saw Stewart's album cover and learned that he was a mere 26 years old, Liebman's response was: "Well the guy's amazing. He sounds like an old cat. You put it on and I thought, this cat's got to be 60 years old. He's beautiful."

In 1996, Stewart recorded what he has referred to as his crowning achievement in the music industry. He is the first Jazz instrumentalist of the 20th century to have recorded the opening chapter of The Holy Qur'an (the sacred scripture of Islam) in music form. He has been known to state that this was his primary reason for becoming a musician and recording artist. The aforementioned track is entitled "Al-Fatihah" (English: The Opening), and the entire recording is entitled "The Force." Stewart's second outing for Quincy Jones' Qwest Records received critical acclaim in the jazz world, for it featured three of the giants of modern jazz: drum icon Jeff "Tain" Watts, bassist extraordinaire Reginald Veal, and piano elder statesman Ed Kelly. Esteemed veteran jazz critic Philip Elwood (of the San Francisco Examiner) wrote: "One doesn't just listen to Stewart's music, one absorbs it." Jazz solo drum founding father Max Roach relays an identical sentiment: "You don't just hear Robert, you FEEL him." Perhaps the most significant of that which has been stated about Stewart (as opposed to other players of his generation) is that he possesses his own unique - distinctive sound. Jazz writer Ezra Gale of the prestigious "Jazz Times Magazine" has stated that Stewart has achieved an intense and personal sound; his solos are remarkably inventive.

In 1999, following the disbanding of the Qwest/Warner Bros. record label by Quincy Jones, Stewart recorded another outing for Red Records entitled "Nat The Cat." This tribute to the vocal icon Nat "King" Cole is the most unique of its kind. Stewart has the uncanny ability to transcend mere notes and chords to create "moods" according to jazz music critic C. Michael Bailey of AllAboutJazz.com. He unconditionally recommends this perfect "mood disc" to all of his readers.

In 2002, Stewart signed for one recording with Exodus Records of Los Angeles entitled "The Movement." The recording is historic for the fact that it was the first reuniting of John Coltrane's original band members (drum legend Billy Higgins and bass legend Dr. Art Davis) since the early 1960's. This live recording also featured bass founding father Al Mckibbon (of Dizzy Gillespie's band) and drum legend Larance Marable (of Charlie Parker's band). This record is also the final band recording of the most recorded drummer in jazz history, Billy Higgins. Billy wrote in the liner notes that Robert Stewart (dubbed "The Reverend" by Wynton Marsalis and his peers) reminded him of John Coltrane himself, and Dexter Gordon. He went on to say that The Reverend (Robert) is "one of the most important artists of his generation and a leader of the new revolution in Jazz."

In 2003, Stewart signed for one recording with the prestigious Nagel-Heyer Records of Germany entitled "Heaven and Earth." This was essentially a "Smooth Jazz" record, and five of the thirteen songs feature Stewart's lyric writing ability. He also makes his debut as a drummer on the final track entitled "Peace Within." The music and lyrics on this album invite one to an elevated spiritual consciousness which is revolutionary in the "Smooth Jazz" idiom. Jazz writer Ronnie D. Lankford Jr. of Allmusic.com eloquently relays this sentiment by stating that there is a positive social message that runs through the songs ("Resolution" and "Peace Within"), and Stewart has found a way to combine new age politics with new age music, creating a hybrid.

In 2006, Stewart released a series of live recordings on Armageddon Records; a label which he co-owned with producer Faheem Al-Azeem. These recordings feature Stewart in live performance with some of the giants of jazz: Pharoah Sanders, Etta Jones, Winard Harper, Mary Stallings, Sonny Simmons, Marcus Printup, Ed Kelly, and others.

Stewart elected to retire from recording and performing (December of 2016) in order to write religious books and pursue his interest in archaeology.

DISCOGRAPHY

LEADER

- Judgement / World Stage Records (1994)

- In The Gutta / Qwest-Warner Bros. Records (1996)

- The Force / Qwest-Warner Bros. Records (1998)

- Beautiful Love Ballads / Red Records (1998)

- Nat The Cat / Red Records (2000)

- The Movement / Exodus Records (2002) featuring Billy Higgins, Dr. Art Davis, Larance Marable, Al McKibbon

- Heaven And Earth / Nagel-Heyer Records (2004)

- Happy Birthday Trane / Armageddon Records (2006) featuring Sonny Simmons

- Invitation / Armageddon Records (2006) featuring Marcus Printup

- Evolution / Armageddon Records (2006) featuring Pharoah Sanders, Etta Jones, Mary Stallings, Winard Harper

- Don't Move The Groove! (Volume 1 - Organ Funk) / Armageddon Records (2006) featuring Ed Kelly

- Don't Move The Groove! (Volume 2 - Organ Blues) / Armageddon Records (2006) featuring Ed Kelly

SIDEMAN

- Ed Kelly & Pharoah Sanders / Evidence Records (1992) Pharoah Sanders, Eddie Marshall

- They Came To Swing / Columbia Records (1994) Wynton, Jon Faddis, Joshua Redman, James Carter, Billy - Higgins, Marcus Roberts, Nicholas Payton, Eric Reed

- Blood On The Fields / Columbia Records (1997) Wynton, Cassandra Wilson, Jon Hendricks, James Carter, Eric Reed, Herlin Riley

- The Music Of America: Wynton Marsalis / Sony Records (2012) Wynton, Harry "Sweets" Edison, Marion Williams

- Can't Hide Love / Seaside Records(1996) Buddy Conner, Wilton Felder, John Handy, Gaylord Birch, Carl Lockett.

- Full Swing Ahead / Deluxe Records (1998) Jay Johnson Mark Shelby Ed Kelly

- Expressions Of A Legacy / Effania Brown Records (2001) Lady Memfis

- Live At Lo Spuntino / Music In The Vines Records (2002) David Leshare Watson

- David Leshare Watson Loves Swining Soft & The Ballads / Music In The Vines Records (2003) David Leshare Watson

COMPILATIONS

- 25th Red Records Anniversary - Un Filo Rosso Nel Jazz / Red Records (2003)

- Red Records : The Color of Jazz / Red Records (2009)

- 30 Jazz Love Standards / Red Records (2010)

- Relaxin Jazz / Red Records (2010)

- Red Records 35th Anniversary / Red Records (2011)

- Ballads 2004 / Nagel-Heyer (2004)

FILMS

- Marsalis On Music Video Series / Columbia Films (1995)

- Sessions At West 54th / PBS Television (1997)

- South Bank Show (Blood On The Fields) / Bravo Television (1995)

Other Books By This Author

Science & Cosmic Messengers

Gender: Issues & Solutions

Islam & Jihad (Holy War) Explained

The Real Mind Of God (A Comparative Scriptural Analysis)

139

Printed in Great Britain
by Amazon

14283691R00081